Everything Is

A Little Bit Alright

Everything Is
A Little Bit Alright

yoga, meditation, and a dog named Roy

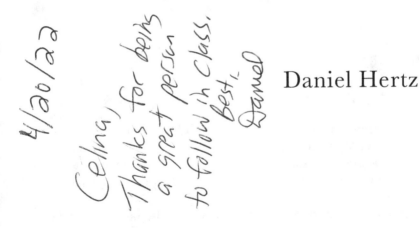

Daniel Hertz

Shanti Arts Publishing
Brunswick, Maine

Published by Shanti Arts Publishing
Interior and cover design by Shanti Arts Designs

Shanti Arts LLC
193 Hillside Road
Brunswick, Maine 04011

shantiarts.com

This is a work of creative nonfiction. The events are portrayed
to the best of the author's memory. While all the stories in
this book are true, some names and identifying details have
been changed to protect the privacy of the people involved.

Photo of the author on cover and page 187 by James Dean Sane.

Printed in the United States of America

ISBN: 978-1-951651-29-9 (softcover)
ISBN: 978-1-951651-30-5 (ebook)

Library of Congress Control Number: 2020937485

May anyone in pain find comfort and love.

Contents

Foreword

by Madelon Sprengnether

YOU ARE ABOUT TO EMBARK ON A WONDERFUL JOURNEY IN reading this book—one that will not only alter the way you think about your life as a whole, but also the way you live it on a day-to-day basis.

I met Daniel in a year-long memoir writing class sponsored by The Loft Literary Center, taught by distinguished fiction writer, memoirist, and children's book author Nicole Helget. Despite my forty-plus years of teaching at the University of Minnesota, I was apprehensive—mainly about switching roles from professor to student—yet also excited. As each of us offered a piece of our work-in-progress, I recall being immediately captured by Daniel's voice: quiet, self-deprecating, funny, honest, and profound. His aim, as I understood it, is to tell us about how he became involved in the practices of yoga and meditation and how they have transformed his life— slowly, and over a very long period of time.

This is neither a sudden conversion narrative nor the kind of self-help book that seems unrealistic in its expectations: "Do this, do that, and your life will change overnight." Rather it is the thoughtful reflection of a person who has lived the story he wants to tell—every step of the way.

I trusted Daniel from the start. He not only does not brag about himself but understates his talents and strengths. Who even does that?

He reports, for instance, each of his failures as a beginning teacher in a sixth grade classroom of unruly students in an underserved Dallas school district, where students are used to physical discipline to keep them in line.

On his very first day, Daniel is confronted by a boy who challenges his authority to his face. "Shut up you white honkey motherfucker!" he shouts. Daniel sends this kid to the principal's office and continues the class lesson, realizing that he needs to develop new strategies for engaging his students. Over time, he finds ways to reach out to them through an effective reward system and by involving their parents (or caregivers) in encouraging their success. By the end of the year, he has a new goal: to certify himself as a math teacher, which he finds easier for his students to master than reading, and to develop his skills as a teacher for underprivileged students. Whereas others might have given up, Daniel not only learns from his experience but persists.

As I read on, I became a witness to Daniel's life struggles: his childhood grief at his parents' divorce when he was too young to cope with the complexity of his emotions; his role as primary caregiver for his mother in her rapid decline and death from lung cancer; and his participation in his father's death only a few years later. Not surprisingly, these experiences had a cumulative effect that manifested (in part) in severe physical pain. Finding his way through this particular torment involves reaching out in many ways—first to an animal companion, who lifts his spirits and leads him outward into the world, and then to a yoga class, where he begins to practice simple body movements accompanied by regular breathing exercises that help not only to relieve his bodily pain but also to open his heart.

I will leave the rest for you to discover, as this journey will move you deeply. Each time I read a new section, I found myself wanting to practice the exercises that Daniel describes.

Each chapter begins with a yoga position that relates to a specific state of body/mind. In this way, Daniel introduces us simply and persuasively to what he discovered in his own practice over the course of many years. His story validates what he is telling us about how he learned to calm his mind and body, come to essential truths about himself and the course of his life (what he calls his "destiny"), and open his mind and heart to love, gratitude, and joy.

Throughout, Daniel admits his own doubts, anxieties, and even failures. This is not a book about relentless upward progress, but rather a deeply honest interrogation into the inner life of a man who wants to understand his history, the choices he has made, and what his life may mean—for himself and others.

You can read this book quickly or slowly. It will reward you either way. It will also repay reading over time, and at different moments in the course of your own life. It's that kind of book.

Everything Is a Little Bit Alright is a work of enduring wisdom.

Madelon Sprengnether
Regents Professor Emerita
Department of English
University of Minnesota

CHAPTER ONE

Living in Panama

BREATHING TO RELAX — Practice the crocodile pose to learn correct diaphragmatic breathing. (Lie on your stomach with the legs a comfortable distance apart and the feet turned out or in. Fold the arms in front of the body, resting the hands on the upper arms, and the forehead on the forearms.)

Nikki started going out to the Canal de Panamá on the weekends for extra fieldwork. She was trying to make up for the missing data on her stolen computer. On a Sunday in early January, 2009, two months after our apartment was robbed and her computer was stolen, she asked me to go along with her. She signed out the Smithsonian pick-up truck and we drove to a remote area of the canal. The guard at the gate required her official ID in order for us to enter the secured area. This ID was issued by the Panama Canal Authority, the agency of the government of Panama responsible for the operation and management of the Panama Canal.

We parked at the end of an empty gravel road.

"Can you stay with the truck?" she asked. "I'll be back in

about twenty minutes." She grabbed her field bag, checked her GPS coordinates, and walked away. After a few steps she disappeared behind the seven-foot-tall elephant grass.

At first I sat in the truck, but even with the windows down, it was too hot. I put on my wide-brimmed sun hat and stood next to the truck in the steaming heat. A noise in the distance caught my attention. I glanced up and saw a large 4-wheel-drive pick-up speeding toward me, kicking up gravel along the way. It skidded to a stop right in front of our truck, blocking it in.

Two guys jumped out and came quickly toward me.

The man on the left looked like the boss since he was two steps ahead of the other one and was barking out instructions in a language I didn't understand. He wore light khaki pants and a green army-style coat. The other guy was thickly built with a shaved head. He wore a black t-shirt and green khaki pants. Both carried *pistolas* on their belts. The leader flashed a badge that I couldn't read and spoke harshly to me in English, in what sounded like an eastern European accent. "Where are your papers?"

"I don't have any papers," I said. If they hadn't blocked in our truck, I may have jumped in and taken off.

"What is your country of origin?" he asked.

"United States," I replied.

"Give me your passport," he demanded.

I took it out and held it tightly in my hand. All thoughts of breath awareness and mantra left me. The adrenaline flowed.

"I said give me the passport." Watching his hand slide slowly toward the pistol convinced me to give it up. He copied down my information in a small notebook.

"What is your business here?" he asked harshly.

"I am a research assistant with the Smithsonian. The scientist is close to here, out in the field." I pointed. "She'll be back shortly." The three of us turned and stared impatiently at the spot I pointed to.

Nikki emerged a minute later from the thick vegetation and walked toward us.

The leader quickly confronted her. "Where are your papers?"

Nikki replied, "I am here on official business." She showed her Canal Authority ID, but did not take it off the lanyard around her neck.

"Give me your passport," the leader demanded.

She didn't budge. "Where is your ID?" she responded.

He flashed it at her like he had to me.

She said firmly, "No, I need to see it."

His assistant had wide eyes and the start of a small smile. He was over a foot taller than Nikki's petite, but sturdy, 5'1" frame, and at least a hundred pounds heavier.

"You have no right to stop me from working," Nikki continued.

The leader said, "You don't know who you are talking to. I will report you first thing tomorrow morning."

Nikki said, "And I will let my supervisor know about you tomorrow morning." She could see my passport in the guy's hand. "Now give my assistant his passport."

He reluctantly handed it back to me.

Nikki whispered, "Daniel, get the camera."

I moved quickly to our truck, grabbed the camera, and snapped pictures of the guys, their truck, and the license plate.

They hurried into their truck and drove away.

I slipped swiftly into the front passenger seat while Nikki jumped into the driver's side. She pulled down the visor to shield her eyes from the sun and drove as fast as the gravel road could handle. After a quarter mile, she pulled the truck over to check and see if anyone followed us. No one was in sight. I could feel my breath slow and shoulders relax.

"Wow, you were amazing," I said. "What do you think that was all about?"

"Who knows?" Nikki replied. She adjusted her side view mirror. "They probably transport all types of weapons and classified stuff on the canal," she said. "Maybe they work security for one of those companies." She loosened her grip on the steering wheel and glanced in the rearview mirror. "Let's get out of here," she said.

※

Two days later I showed up to the Smithsonian Library for the next meditation class. I greeted Arturo, the librarian who had organized the meditation class that I was leading. As usual, I set up the chairs for the students. Then I sat down and closed my eyes in meditation practice for ten minutes before the students arrived. The class started at the regular 5:00 pm time. "Any questions today, Arturo?" I asked.

"Yes, here's one," he said. "No matter what I try, I can't relax. Please help."

The canal incident immediately came to mind, but when I paused to slow my breath, another thought took its place. "I've had that feeling many times before," I told the class. "When I was diagnosed ten years ago with a hyperthyroid condition, the guided relaxations and meditations just made it worse. My heart would start pounding every time I tried to quiet down." The marine biologist, a student in the class, came in late and I waited for him to sit down. "When you want to relax and nothing else works, I have found this practice to be very effective. It sounds simple, but it is very powerful. You can experiment with it to see if it works for you."

Another student, the human resources director, perked up. "Please tell us."

"Make the exhalation longer than the length of the inhalation. The exhalation activates the parasympathetic, or relaxation side, of the nervous system. For example, if you are inhaling four seconds, exhale for five or six seconds. Or, if possible, double the exhalation to eight seconds." I stopped talking and watched as they tried it. The accountant strained on the exhalation. "Remember to combine this with the diaphragmatic breathing and to keep the breath effortless, without forcing anything."

On the walk back to our apartment after class that night, the canal incident still weighed heavily on my mind. I reminded myself why we had come to Panama in the first place. A year earlier, on a freezing February day in 2008, Nikki had told me that her post-doc application for a year-long job in Panama was accepted. The Smithsonian Tropical Research Institute in Panama City needed someone with her background in sedimentary geology. The research institute was a world leader in the study of tropical ecosystems, their evolution through time, their future, and their relevance to human welfare. This was an amazing opportunity for Nikki, and it meant a lot to her.

Getting out of Minneapolis for the next winter sounded like a great idea. I immediately applied for a leave from my school counselor job with the Minneapolis Public Schools. We started to plan all the cumbersome details for our move to Panama.

※

Seven months before that canal incident, in July 2008, I walked off the plane at midnight in Panama City and hit a wall of heat and humidity. Nikki saw me in the baggage claim and ran toward me. She had come to Panama two weeks earlier to start her geology post-doc with the Smithsonian while I had stayed in Minneapolis to wrap up some loose ends with my job and the house.

"Welcome to Panama," she said. We embraced and she pulled me close. Even though she was smaller than me in size, her presence of light and goodness loomed large. The familiar feeling of intimacy washed over me. We had been married for four years.

Nikki hauled one of my duffel bags as she led me to the waiting taxi.

The driver loaded my bags in the trunk. "Forty-five minute ride. *Vamonos a la jaula,*" said the driver. We slid in the backseat.

"*La jaula?*" I asked Nikki.

"The dormitory is nicknamed *la jaula,*" she said.

"*La jaula*" is translated to English as "the jail." Nikki explained that there were steel bars on the windows and a chain-link fence surrounded the open-air hallways. The dorm was located in a tropical rainforest called Ancon on the largest hill in Panama City.

When I opened my window in the taxi to get a better view of the Pacific Ocean and the downtown skyline, the heat flowed in. The AC helped to dry some of the sweat rolling off of me. I found a clean paper towel in the pocket of my cargo pants and blotted my face.

Nikki's post-doctoral work was part of a huge effort to quickly map the geology of the canal area during the Panama Canal expansion project.

"What do they actually have you do?" I asked. Nikki and I had talked on the phone several times since she left, but mostly it was about details on what to bring and the crazy weather.

"Mostly doing a lot of fieldwork on the canal right now." She smiled and nodded at me. "It's really interesting stuff." Her voice rose with excitement. "Climate change. Biodiversity. A lot of things."

The taxi dropped us off. Before entering our second-floor room, I set my bags down in front of the door. Nikki and I looked outside through the chain link fence lining the hallway. Although it was dark, we could still see the surrounding grounds by the light of the moon. The stifling musty smell hung in the air.

"I can't believe we're here for a year," I said. The Pacific entrance to the canal was only a fifteen-minute walk.

"Well, we will have to find a real apartment after two months. These rooms are only meant to be temporary," Nikki replied. This information was new to me.

A little animal running on the grass in front of us caught my eye.

"Whoa, what was that?" I asked.

"I don't know what they are called, but they are kind of like the squirrels at home. All over the place."

"It looks like a combination of a giant rat and rabbit," I said.

She laughed. "There are all sorts of strange creatures around here. After dark, a three-toed sloth is sometimes hanging in a tree, up that hill."

I took out my handkerchief and wiped the sweat from my forehead. Other dorm residents entered the gate below us.

"And every morning so far I have seen a toucan high in the trees," she said. "Right behind here."

Nikki took out her key and opened the dorm room. There was a bed, bathroom, narrow closet, galley kitchen, and small kitchen table. The cold air was a welcome relief. A small lizard poked its head out from behind the wall clock.

"Do you kind of get used to that thing staring at you?" I asked.

"Yeah, I think every room has at least one gecko." Nikki set down my suitcase. "He keeps to himself. A kind of low-maintenance pet."

We sat at the kitchen table and held hands. The warmth of her hand was soothing after a long day of travel, and I could feel my shoulders relax. Her shoulder-length brown hair framed her pretty, roundish face and green eyes. She was tan and keeping fit from the daily fieldwork. "I hope you will be OK here spending a lot of time on your own," Nikki said. Her work would require long hours and probably some time at remote locations away from Panama City.

My shoulders tensed. "A few days ago I talked to the international school down here," I told her. I had been in touch with them about a job opening.

"And?" she asked.

"When I told them I was only interested in part-time, they weren't too excited."

"OK, well, I met the librarian on the Smithsonian campus," she said. He told Nikki they have been looking for someone to teach yoga and meditation after the workday.

The tension in my shoulders released as I slowly exhaled. "Oh, cool, maybe I can catch him tomorrow."

"If you decide to do that, it is about a half mile this way." She pointed. "Opposite direction of the fruit market." The largest fruit and vegetable market in the city was only a ten-minute walk from our dorm room.

Nikki fell asleep quickly that night. As I lay in bed, thoughts flowed through my mind. So much had happened in the last few days. There were so many details to take care of. Our house had to be completely emptied out for the renter. My job as a school counselor was very busy. And saying goodbye to friends seemed endless. On top of all that, we also got word that our good friend, Swami Hari, had passed away in India. I attended a poignant remembrance ceremony for him at the Meditation Center in Minneapolis a few days before. In my fifty-one years, I had never met anyone like him. Then sleep swept me away.

Early the next morning, Nikki had to go to her job. Her work routine started at her office, which was a short walk up the hill from the dorm. After taking a few minutes to load equipment into the van, her research team would then head out to the canal. An early start meant fieldwork in the oppressive humidity, but at least they escaped the sweltering heat of the afternoon sun. In the afternoons and evenings, she returned to the research lab to input and organize the field data.

Before leaving, she again pointed me toward the fruit and

vegetable market. Then she pointed in the opposite direction, to the campus where the library was located.

The vegetation along the way to the market was green, lush, thick, and tropical. There were many species of trees and plants that I did not recognize. After a few steps, a large iguana sped past me. My eyes tracked where it went, and several yards away it gathered up a few baby iguanas on the nearby grass. The houses I passed all had bars on the windows, just like *la jaula*. After three blocks, I was drenched in sweat.

About half-way to the market, huge streaks of lightening appeared on the horizon. Ominous bloated clouds towered high and thick. Loud claps of thunder vibrated all around me. The warm rain came hard and fast. Out of habit I started to walk faster and then slowed back down to my usual pace. Since I was already completely soaked and it was an outdoor market, what was the point of rushing? By the time I made it to the market a few minutes later, the rain had stopped. Panama City averaged over ten feet of rain a year, but this downpour was more intense than I could have imagined.

The vendors used US dollars, and you could bargain a little if buying in bulk, but mostly they told you the price and that was it. There was booth after booth filled with avocados, papayas, melons, plantains, bananas, mangoes, and much more. One section had a sea of pineapples laid out on wooden pallets in an area the size of a football field. My backpack was quickly filled with a variety of fruits, and I walked back to our new home. I couldn't wait to try the pineapple. As soon as I got the door open, I found a knife in the kitchen drawer and cut it up. The sweet, juicy chunks melted in my mouth, and I finished the whole thing. After the snack, I changed into dry clothes, made sure to pack my umbrella, and headed to the library.

My shirt was again soaked from sweat after a few blocks. Two blocks from the library, the rain started again. Even though I got my umbrella open in time, the wind was so strong it blew the rain sideways, under the umbrella. I found the library and walked in soaking wet. In the entranceway I tried to brush off the extra water from my hair and clothes.

A stout, smiling guy about forty years old greeted me from behind the counter. "*Cómo puedo ayudarle?* How can I help you?"

"How does someone stay dry in this weather?" I asked.

He laughed. "It's not easy, but you learn to figure it out."

"My wife, Nikki, told me to ask for Arturo."

"That's me, *mucho gusto*, nice to meet you."

We shook hands.

Someone else was trying to get his attention at the counter.

"*Un momento,*" he told me. He had a calm demeanor and a sparkle in his eye.

When he returned to me, I mentioned what Nikki had said about him looking for a yoga and meditation teacher. Before leaving Minneapolis, I did a Google search and only found three or four registered yoga teachers in all of Panama City. No meditation teachers were listed.

I took out a few soaked pieces of paper and handed them to him. "Here are my credentials. Sorry about the water."

"It's OK, I can still read it." He flipped through them. "So you are certified in yoga, meditation, and biofeedback?"

"That's correct." Since 1995 I had been giving classes at the Meditation Center in Minneapolis. The center was part of the worldwide Himalayan Yoga and Meditation Tradition, which included gentle hatha yoga and sitting meditation.

"What do you have in mind for the classes?" I asked.

Another customer was waiting for him at the counter.

"*Un momento,*" he said again.

He returned a minute later. "We have a group of ten or fifteen employees who are interested in studying after work, maybe two days a week."

"That's great," I said.

"Do you want to try it next Tuesday, 5 o'clock, and see how it goes?" he asked.

❈

For the first meditation class, I got to the library fifteen minutes early and spread out four rows of chairs, with four in each row. The large windows in the library let in plenty of natural light, so I turned off the overhead lights. Since Panama was near the equator, the sunset time was always close to 6:00 pm, the same time the hour-long class ended.

Arturo advertised the class through an email and word of mouth. Now all we had to do was wait to see if anyone would show up. Sharing what I learned from my meditation practice always made me feel like I was making good use of my time. Life goes fast and our time is limited. Making a positive contribution to the world was what I wanted to do more than anything else.

As the class participants entered the library, I introduced myself and asked them about their work. About half were research scientists like Nikki, and the others worked on the administrative side of the Smithsonian. A couple of the scientists wore jeans, but the others had changed into sweatsuit-style workout clothes.

When everyone was seated, I began. "*Bienvenido a la clase a todos*. Welcome everyone." I looked at Arturo. "Does everyone speak English?"

Most nodded.

Arturo said, "Everyone does. If they find a word they don't understand, they will ask if someone can translate." That was a relief. Before leaving Minneapolis I studied some key Spanish words related to meditation, but using them quickly and smoothly would have been a struggle.

"Great, please sit on the front half of the chair, with your back straight and feet firmly planted on the ground." I remained in my chair and modeled what I wanted them to do. "See how I am sitting? Upright but not stiff." I reminded myself to speak slowly and pronounce each word clearly. "Close your eyes and find your breath. See if you can follow the breath from where it enters the body to where it exits."

Before closing my eyes, I looked around the room. Of the thirteen people, seven were women. The marine biologist sat in the middle of the second row, loudly blowing his nose. The accountant looked tired and was slumped in her third row chair, the entomologist sat in back and was putting away a book, and the maintenance manager was sitting upright in the front row, ready to go. The botanist also sat in the back row. She was the oldest of the group by far and looked to be in her seventies. Student number fourteen entered the library, and I waited as she took a seat in the back row.

"Stay with me, everyone. Please keep your attention at the point between the nostrils. If possible, breathe in and out of your nose."

The entomologist raised his hand. "Why breathe in and out of the nose?"

"It is a finer instrument for feeling the movement of the air," I said. "It also warms and cleanses the air you bring into your body."

"My nose is plugged," said the marine biologist.

"It is OK to use your mouth until your nose clears up," I replied.

"Now, start to count the length of your exhalation, silently, as in 1-1000, 2-1000, 3-1000, 4-1000, 5-1000," I said. "If possible, *exhalando cinco segundos*, exhaling for five seconds; *inhalando cinco segundos*, inhaling for five seconds. The same length in each direction." We sat in silence for a few minutes. "Please don't force the breathing. Be very gentle with yourself. If five seconds is too long, start with three or four seconds. Keep the count going." We continued to sit in silence for a few more minutes. Sitting together in silence was a supportive way to help the students notice the subtle meditative state.

"A comforting way to end a meditation practice is to keep your eyes closed and rub your hands together until they are warm." I demonstrated with the sound of my rubbing hands, and the others joined in. "Now please open your eyes into the warmth of your palms." The botanist took off her glasses. They all had their palms over their eyes.

They lowered their hands and looked at me.

"Next class, please remember to bring a blanket or mat," I announced. "We will do some gentle stretching and also lay on the floor for a guided relaxation."

After class, the woman who came in late stopped to introduce herself. "Hi, I'm the human resources director here. Sorry I was late to the class." We shook hands. "We are having a Health Fair next week."

"Sounds interesting," I said.

"Arturo tells me you are also a biofeedback practitioner. How would you like to have a display at the fair where you could demonstrate what it is?"

"That would be great."

The next morning I returned to the fruit and vegetable market. I craved another sweet and juicy pineapple. The potassium in the pineapple helped maintain a balance of the electrolytes in my body from all the sweating.

The following weekend Nikki took a break from work. We caught a short taxi ride to the Casco Viejo section of the city. The seventeenth-century Spanish colonial architecture had been beautifully restored and it became a World Heritage Site in 1997. We strolled along the waterfront and enjoyed a great view of the city skyline.

A couple of days later, the Health Fair was held in a building near the library. The large room had open space in the middle, and tables lined the walls so people could walk around and see all the displays. My name was on a sign on one of the tables. Next to my name were the words *Biorretroalimentación* and Biofeedback. There was a basic Biofeedback program on my laptop. I sat down, opened it up, and looked around. Next to me was a nurse checking blood pressure. On the other side was a display and information on diabetes.

Employees moved through the room and stopped at the displays that caught their attention. The maintenance manager from the meditation class sat down at my table. "What is this all about?" he asked.

"If I put this clip on your earlobe, your heart rate will show up on the computer screen. Do you want to try it?"

"*Bueno.*"

"See how the line is jagged?"

"*Sí.*"

"OK, now sit up straight and slow your breathing to this rate." I turned on the pacer and set it to five seconds in each direction. "Inhale as the bar goes up and exhale as it comes down."

He started to slow his breath to the rate of the pacer.

"The key is allowing yourself to relax rather than trying," I told him. "Trying creates tension."

He followed the pacer for three minutes. "See how the line has smoothed out?" I asked.

He nodded. "*Sí.*"

The line was also moving up and down. The heart rate naturally went up on the inhalation and down on the exhalation.

"The variability in your heart rate is getting wider." I pointed to it on the graph. This indicated a greater ability to respond to the myriad of stressors we face everyday. In times of stress, the sympathetic side, or fight/flight side, of the autonomic nervous system takes over and the heart rate variability shrinks. When a person is relaxed, the parasympathetic side of the nervous system is activated and the heart rate variability increases.

"Do you feel more relaxed?" I asked.

He smiled, stood up slowly, and nodded his head. "I think so. *Gracias.*"

The day after the Health Fair we finished up the second week of meditation classes.

When everyone was seated, I began. "Is it OK if we start each class with questions?" Arturo and I had spoken before the class. He already had two questions someone emailed to him earlier in the week. "How much should I practice?" he read.

"It's important to practice everyday," I replied. "The amount of time is not important. Two minutes a day is enough for a start." How you practice is much more important than how much you practice.

The entomologist was sitting in back again. He looked up from the book he was reading. "Where is the best place to practice?"

"Find a comfortable place at a convenient time. Quiet is better, but if it gets noisy, no problem, just keep going."

The accountant was in the front row. She didn't look as tired as she had at the first class. "Practice everyday?" she asked.

"Meditation is a new skill that you are learning. If you want to learn to play the piano, would it help to practice everyday?"

Several people nodded.

"If you practice meditation everyday, not just when you feel like it, it can reverberate throughout your life." I glanced back at Arturo. He was still looking expectantly at me. "For example," I added, "it has helped me to both focus my attention and learn to relax."

"Second question, how long will it take to feel the benefits of meditation?" Arturo said.

"The time to learn meditation is now, when things in your life are going OK. Meditation can help you in a crisis, but it is very difficult to learn it in the middle of a crisis," I said. I sat up straight, closed my eyes, and slowly let out the air on my exhalation. My eyes opened and I looked at the students. "Release any expectations of what it will or won't do." I smiled. "This is how I look at it: By sitting quietly for a few minutes a day, at least you're not adding to the crazy, angry turmoil out there."

In August of 2008, the US presidential election between Obama and McCain was kicking into high gear. At the same time, Panama was in the middle of their own intense presidential election. Our dorm room at *la jaula* was located only three blocks away from the Supreme Court building. The start of my daily walk up Ancon Hill took me by the large, raucous, daily protests outside the court building. During the protests, someone yelled rapid fire Spanish that I didn't understand into a megaphone while people chanted and held up signs. Whenever I passed by the protest, I sped up my walking pace so I wouldn't accidentally get caught up in the mess when the police arrived.

The end of August arrived quickly, and I had already been in Panama for six weeks.

"Will you be OK on your own during the time I'm gone?" Nikki asked. She would be away on the research vessel RV Urraca for three weeks. Most of their time would be spent in the remote Kuna Yala region on the Caribbean side of the country. I was standing at our kitchen counter, chopping some vegetables for dinner. She came up from behind and gave me a tight hug.

That put a smile on my face. "Well, I think I can survive." I knew how to take a taxi to the grocery store.

She sat back down at the table and started to read a flier I had set there. "You're getting busier," she said. Several people had already responded to the fliers I posted advertising English lessons.

"Plus," Nikki said, "You know some people in the dorm now, to hang out with."

I nodded.

"I leave in three days," she said.

They arranged for me and the other spouses to come along for the first day as the boat traveled through the canal to the other side of the country.

The Panama Canal was built in 1914 and operated by the United States until 1979. At that time Panama gradually started to run it until they completely took it over on the last day of 1999. Some 14,000 ships from all over the world pass through the canal every year.

The boat ride across the canal took ten to twelve hours. It gave me a chance to meet some of Nikki's colleagues. Everyone was very interested in watching the huge cargo ships passing close to our small research vessel. And all of us were fascinated by the details of the multi-chamber lock systems we passed through.

The cook on the boat made lunch for everyone. When Nikki and I told him we were vegetarians, he didn't look happy. *How would Nikki find enough food to eat during her three-week trip?* He brought out a couple scoops of bland rice and beans for Nikki and me while the others enjoyed their shredded beef and coconut rice.

After the boat reached the Caribbean side, I joined the six spouses and partners for the fifty-mile train ride back to Panama City. I sat next to a herpetologist from Germany. He and his paleontologist wife had been in Panama for a year and owned a car. He said he would come by the next weekend and show me some of the places around town that I hadn't seen yet.

The boat ride across the canal and train ride back took all day, and I returned to the dorm late in the evening. As I opened the door to our room, I heard a loud crash inside. After turning on a light, I did a quick scan of the room. The clock on the wall had fallen to the floor. My roommate for the next three weeks was standing on the wall where the clock had been, looking very guilty. "Come on," I said. "We have to get along for the next three weeks. If Nikki comes back and finds the place trashed, she'll be very upset." When I smiled toward the gecko and held out my hand, I thought I detected a small nod before he scampered off to his new hiding place behind the framed picture on the wall.

Everyone arrived on time at the next meditation class. Arturo had a question ready to go. "The second I sit down and close my eyes, I lose track of my breathing and start daydreaming. Is that meditation?"

"The two biggest fallacies about meditation are that . . . "

The botanist interrupted me. "*Qué significa la falacia?*" Arturo explained to the group in Spanish what fallacy meant and I continued.

"Number one, meditation is not daydreaming or spacing out. It is a very focused activity." I paused to look at all the students and could see through the large windows that the rain had started again. "Fallacy number two," I held up two fingers, "it is not emptying the mind. The stream of thoughts can slow down when you change the focus of the mind, but the mind still needs to be focused on something. If you can follow one . . . " I held up a finger. "Just one exhalation, from start to finish, without a thought, you have accomplished something very big. That becomes the building block for your meditation practice."

The first week Nikki was out of town, I found some people from the dorm to join for lunch. A group of us also went out to a movie on the weekend. They were very nice, but it wasn't the same as hanging out with old friends. Loneliness started to creep in.

During the second week, I spent time on the Internet checking out some of the ex-pat Yahoo user groups. At least 20,000 former US citizens lived in Panama. The ex-pats posted helpful tips on places to eat and shop, which neighborhoods to avoid, and how to deal with the taxi drivers. Taxi rides to anywhere in the city were under five dollars. Nikki and I used taxis as our main form of transportation. The drivers talked so fast that they were difficult to understand. Due to the tips from the ex-pats, I got better at giving directions to them in Spanish.

During Nikki's third week away, I found a letter taped outside the door of our dorm room. In very strict terms, it said we needed to vacate our dorm room by the end of the month. We were responsible for finding our own housing. This left us only ten days to find a place and move out.

When I posted online to an ex-pat Yahoo group that we were looking for an apartment in the Ancon area, I only got one response. The man wrote that apartments were impossible to find there because it was such a popular area for both Panamanians and employees of the Smithsonian. Everywhere I walked I kept my eyes open for apartments to rent, but didn't see a thing.

After almost three months of living in Panama, seeing and learning new things everyday was still exciting. But I missed Nikki's love and inspiration while she was away, and the constant newness of everything started to wear me down.

The day after Nikki returned from her research trip, we went to talk to the housing administrator. She told us that new researchers were coming everyday, and they needed a place to stay, just like we did. I explained that I had been looking, but with no luck.

"Do you have any suggestions on places to stay?" I asked.

"I'm sorry," said the housing administrator. "This is a big institution and we have a lot of people coming and going."

"If you can't help us find a place, can you at least give us an extension?" Nikki asked. "I've been away for the last three weeks on a research project."

She relented and gave us a thirty-day extension on the dorm lease.

That same week I got an email asking me to call the dean of the international school I had been in touch with a few months before. They had a new sixth-grade teacher who was having some classroom management issues and asked me if I would be interested in coming in to mentor him for two hours every morning. I made plans for the following week to visit the school and meet the principal.

Meanwhile, at the next meditation class, Arturo read this question: "What does he mean when he says diaphragmatic breathing?"

"Diaphragmatic breathing is the type you do while practicing meditation," I said. "It is a deeper breathing, in the area of your lower ribcage." I stood up and demonstrated. "A test of diaphragmatic breathing is if the bottom of your rib cage flares slightly out to the side on the inhalation."

"But why do we need to breathe like this?" Arturo asked.

"When we are stressed, our natural reaction is to move to shallow, quicker, chest breathing. Diaphragmatic breathing activates the relaxation response." The vagus nerve travels through the diaphragm and is associated with the parasympathetic or relaxation side of the nervous system.

"Please come to the upright position in your chair," I said. I sat down with them. "The upright position allows for a free movement of the diaphragm."

When everyone was seated properly, I continued. "Now place your hands at your side, where the ribcage ends." I stood up again to show them where I put my hands. "Can you feel the ribcage flare out on the inhalation?"

The botanist shook her head. "The only thing I can feel is the weight I need to lose." A few people laughed.

I walked to the back row where she was sitting and smiled. "Let's have a look," I said.

She tried it.

"I can see your shoulders rise on the inhalation," I told her. "Try to keep the shoulders and chest still."

The botanist frowned.

"Not to worry," I said. "It can take some time to learn, but it is worth it." I came back to the front of the room and demonstrated again. "Make a point of bringing your awareness to that area throughout the day, whenever you remember to check."

On Monday morning of the following week I took a taxi out to the international school for the interview.

Nikki got back to our dorm room at 5:00 pm. "How did it go?" she asked.

"They want me to start next week."

"Serious?"

"Yup. The job seems interesting." The teachers were energetic and welcoming.

I lifted the lid and checked on the rice I was making for dinner. "Someone at the school told me they have the largest kosher grocery store in the world here—outside of Tel Aviv."

"Cool, let's take a look at it, maybe next Sunday?" Nikki asked.

I nodded. "Hopefully, whichever taxi we find will know how to get there."

Nikki checked the refrigerator to see what vegetables we had on hand. "Will you take the job?" she asked.

I was already busy with the meditation classes and English tutoring. Plus, I wanted to do some volunteer work with Nikki on the canal. "I'll try it, see how it goes."

☀

The meditation classes had been going on twice a week, Tuesdays and Thursdays, from 5:00 to 6:00 pm, for over three months. Everyone knew the routine. They dropped off two dollars in the donation bowl on the way in, then found a chair and set up their yoga mat next to it. Often people would relax on the mat until class started. Every class began with a guided relaxation and gentle stretching on the mat, and I would take any questions once they were seated in the chair.

"OK, Arturo, any questions today?" I asked.

"Here's one: Sometimes when I am sitting, difficult thoughts come into my mind, and I feel like running away. What can I do?"

"Run as fast as you can!" I responded.

They laughed.

"I ran away from my meditation cushion many times," I continued. "When difficult thoughts come into your mind, release the areas of bodily tension, like we have been practicing in the guided relaxations. And especially remember to breathe slowly."

The maintenance manager nodded from his usual front row seat and closed his eyes.

"Be gentle and forgiving of yourself. Try smiling to yourself." I stopped talking and made an exaggerated smile. "That is how I remind myself to remain light-hearted in the challenging times."

Arturo greeted someone at the library entrance who wanted to try out the class for the first time. The new student settled down in the back row and sat up in the chair like the other students.

"Remember to be nice to yourself," I reminded them. Falling into a negative chain of thoughts was common in meditation, especially when first learning it. "Let's try it together."

I sat up in my chair and closed my eyes.

After ten minutes of sitting, the marine biologist interrupted the silence. "But the thoughts, what about the thoughts?"

"Follow the process, and you will find every thought eventually dissipates, no matter how intense it seems." I could see the marine biologist open his eyes wide. "Don't push the thought away," I said. "Don't pull it in." My eyes closed. "Simply witness the thoughts without judgment, and then return to the task at hand, which is to slow your breath, find your point of focus, and relax your body." I opened my eyes and looked at the group. Everyone had their eyes closed. "This is the process of meditation," I said. "And it repeats, over and over again."

In mid-October, the entomologist stopped to talk with me after class. He had finished his research project and was going back to his university position in New Mexico. This meant he would be vacating his two bedroom apartment that was within walking distance to Nikki's work. I immediately jumped on it.

The next day the entomologist introduced me to his landlord and then left us alone. When I asked a question about lease length and monthly rent, I realized he did not speak any English. Fortunately, my basic Spanish was enough to figure it out. We moved in during the last week of October.

The apartment was in a large, old, wooden fourplex-style building. The US Army Corps of Engineers designed and built it while they were still managing the canal. The building had extra long, overhanging eaves. This allowed the large bar-less screen windows to remain open in the second-floor apartment, even in the heavy rains. There were air conditioners in the bedrooms, but no AC in the living room, dining room, or kitchen. This meant the air was very hot and humid in those rooms. I left a backpack in the same spot on the living room floor for the first three days; when I turned it over, green mold was already starting to form.

A week after we moved into our new apartment, on November 4, 2008, we had a combination housewarming / election night party for about a dozen people. We thought it would be a late night, but by 11:00 pm, Obama easily had enough electoral votes.

When I arrived for class on Thursday, Arturo had already set up the chairs.

"I had a few extra minutes," he said.

As each student arrived, they unrolled their mat and laid down in *savasana*, the relaxation posture on their back, while waiting for the class to start. I led the class in a few simple yoga stretches for about ten minutes.

Everyone took a seat.

"No questions today," Arturo said.

"It is already the beginning of November," I said. "We have been practicing meditation together for the last several months." We started with fourteen students, six dropped out, but four more joined along the way, so a total of twelve were attending the classes regularly. Turnover like this is common in meditation classes. Many people try meditation but few establish a daily practice. Even fewer make it a lifetime practice. My daily practice started fifteen years earlier, in 1993.

"About two months ago, I mentioned that there needs to be a focus of the mind. So far we have focused on the breath and the point between the nostrils." The human resources director said, "Focusing on the breath works for me."

"Some people focus on the breath for their whole life's practice, so that may be enough for you," I responded. "But you can also focus on a point on the body, like the heart center." I pointed to my heart area. "You can also count your breaths. If you are repeating a mantra, you can count the mantra repetitions."

"A mantra?" the maintenance manager asked.

"It is a sacred word that you repeat silently in your mind. A gentle, balancing mantra to start with is to silently repeat the word 'So' on the inhalation and 'Hum' on the exhalation." In the Himalayan Tradition, one practice is to focus your meditation on all four things simultaneously: breath, point of focus, mantra, and counting the repetitions of the mantra.

We were running a little over time with class and a couple of people got up to leave. "If you can wait for one more minute, I'll be done."

They sat down.

"Thank you for your patience everyone. If anything I've said tonight seems too complicated or overwhelming, *no te preocupes*, not to worry. For now, go back to the basics. Bring your focus back to the breath. Silently say 'out' on the exhalation and 'in' on the inhalation. We'll review the other stuff next week."

☀

Three weeks after moving into the apartment, early on a mid-November morning, I came out of the air-conditioned bedroom. My jeans were on the floor. As I picked them up to check for mold, I noticed my wallet was gone.

"Nikki!" I shouted. "My wallet is missing. Have you seen it?"

"No, I don't have it." She came out of the bedroom and searched the dining room table where she had worked the night before. "What?! My computer is gone," she said.

I glanced at the screen on the back window. It was jarred loose. In a panic, I got dressed, went quickly outside, and found two policemen standing on a nearby corner.

"*Sargento, un ladrón robo nuestro apartamento.* A thief robbed our apartment. Very close to here." I pointed.

They followed me to the apartment, interviewed us, and took notes for over an hour. Nikki served them cookies and tea, and they seemed more interested in Nikki and the cookies than what

I was saying. Before leaving, they looked out the back screen window and pointed to some barefooted prints in the mud below.

Nikki had to get to work so I was on my own with the policemen.

The officers asked me to follow them to the main police station for all of Panama City. It was on the way to the fruit and vegetable market, only a ten minute walk from our apartment. When we arrived at the station, they pointed me in the direction of the detective's office. The secretary greeted me, "*Buenos días*, good morning."

"*Buenas*," I said quickly. "Our apartment was robbed this morning. The two officers behind me have all the information."

"What officers?" she asked.

When I turned around, they were gone. I ran out the door to find them, but they were nowhere in sight, so I returned to the office.

After an hour's wait, a detective came out and brought me to his office down the hall. I told him the whole story, including what the two police officers did.

"That sergeant and his friend are *idiotas*," he said. "Talking with them was a waste of time." He typed something on his computer. "You are lucky you didn't run into the thief last night in your apartment. He might have slit your throat."

I raised my eyebrows in disbelief.

"I am totally serious," he said. "We had a case like that a few weeks ago, in this same neighborhood."

"Oh, boy," I replied. My mind was buzzing with what to do next.

"The thief may come back again," he continued. "To them, you are the new candy store on the block. I am afraid your two hundred dollars and your wife's computer are long gone."

Now what do we do? Move out today? Why did I come to Panama? Maybe we should go back to Minneapolis, like now.

He handed me an official police report.

On the walk back to the apartment, I could feel the tension in my forehead and a tightness in my heart no matter how much I slowed my breath.

The landlord was home, and I told him what happened. "*Nunca, nunca, nunca*. Never before has this happened," he said. He promised to install bars on the windows as soon as he could. He also said he would keep his dog outside all night to scare away any intruders. His assurances helped ease my mind a bit. I hoped he was telling the truth about putting bars on the windows.

I called our credit union in Minneapolis, canceled my debit card, and ordered a new one. I also went online and requested a new driver's license. It would take weeks to get them. First they would have to be mailed to our address in Minneapolis, then our neighbor in Minneapolis who was collecting our mail would have to send them to Panama.

At dinner that night, I told Nikki everything the landlord and detective had said.

"All the field data I've collected for the last five months was on that computer," she said.

"It was backed up, right?" I asked.

"Just some of it," she said.

My heart skipped a beat.

"I need a hug," she said.

"Me too."

Before going into the bedroom that night, we locked all the windows. Then we brought all the cash we had left, our passports, and my laptop into bed with us. I propped a chair under the bedroom door handle so it couldn't be opened from the other side. Earlier in the day I found a one-foot-long two-by-four board in back of the building. I put it underneath the bed as a kind of security weapon.

The landlord's dog barked all night long and woke both of us up several times. Each time I woke up, I stayed awake until I was sure no one was in the apartment. The feelings of fear and anxiety rushing through my mind nullified any positive effects of the slow breathing I was trying to do.

On the way to class the next day, the sun was shining bright. I was a few minutes late. Everyone was laying on their mats when I arrived. I sat in silence for a few minutes then led them through a guided relaxation.

When everyone was seated, Arturo read the first question. "How do you cultivate positive emotions?"

"You don't turn on a switch and all of a sudden become a positive person," I answered.

Someone opened up the library door and yelled. "Are you still open?"

We all ignored it and the person left.

"It takes a constant vigilance of watching your emotions, and if possible, reframing them to something positive," I said. "For example, when your mind wanders during meditation and you notice it has wandered, bring it back to the task at hand. Rather than being upset that it has wandered, be grateful you had the awareness to notice that it did wander."

I took out my bandanna and wiped the sweat from my forehead. The library was air-conditioned, but I was still warm from the walk over. "Some of you may have heard, our apartment was recently robbed." A few people nodded. "The easiest thing for me to do is to settle into anger and resentment. Part of me wants to get out of Panama as fast as I can." Since the robbery, I had urged myself over and over to focus on the positive. The main thing was that we were not physically harmed.

The accountant asked, "*Señor* Daniel, even though you've been practicing meditation for a long time, do you still get stressed out in these difficult situations?"

"*Por supuesto*. Of course. The robbery is still heavy in my mind and heart. When something like this happens, you feel violated and disappointed in humanity." I could feel myself holding back a tear.

"No matter how long you study and practice, you are always a student with a lot to learn," I said. "At least now I have some techniques and strategies to use to deal with it. I don't feel quite as helpless to the whim of whatever the wind blows my way."

After class, the accountant, human resources manager, and botanist all came up to say they were sorry about the break-in. They asked me if we were OK and had everything we needed. Their caring and concern helped a lot.

By early January, two months had passed since our apartment was robbed. As promised, our landlord installed steel bars on the windows. I started to feel comfortable living in Panama, and my doubts about staying there had all but disappeared. Then the incident on the canal with the *pistolas* happened. and it brought back all those doubts and fears.

What helped move me beyond doubt and fear after the canal incident was that starting in mid-January, we had almost continuous visits from friends and relatives. Our two-bedroom apartment was big enough to house them, and I was happy to show them all the sights around town. The familiar company was enough to take the edge off any lingering feelings of loneliness and questioning why we were there.

On January 20 of 2009, Nikki and I, along with two old friends visiting from Minneapolis, watched the inauguration of President Obama on television. Even though we were four thousand miles away, we could sense the excitement in the air. As the cameras scanned the audience, the announcers said there were more people in attendance than for any previous event held in Washington, DC. The idealism and sense of a new start was contagious.

The next day I smiled when the Panamanian security guard at the Smithsonian said, *'Si, se puede'* (Yes, we can) when he saw me. That was a slogan of the Obama campaign.

By February of that year, the great recession of 2009 was in full force, and any university job openings that fit Nikki's background became very scarce. Because of that, we made the decision to return to Minneapolis at the end of her year-long Smithsonian contract. We notified our house renter in Minneapolis that we would be returning July 1. I withdrew my leave with the Minneapolis Public Schools and interviewed to get my old job back at Wellstone International High School. During the long distance phone interview, I sat outside surrounded by palm trees, while the subzero winds were whipping up snow around Minneapolis.

By March, after eight months of living in Panama, I finally felt adjusted to the searing heat and humidity. Being in an air-conditioned room felt too cold. I preferred to sleep under a slow-moving ceiling fan. Eating fresh fruit everyday became a habit. Drinking coconut water or eating a pineapple were both very effective in restoring the electrolyte balance from all the sweating. I had bought so much fresh fruit since arriving in Panama that I became an expert on how many days it would take for any particular type of fruit to be at peak ripeness.

In April and May we settled into a routine, without any

pistolas or thieves. There were no more out-of-town visitors. Nikki did what she could to wrap up her research, and I finished my job at the school. Panama felt very familiar and, to my surprise, started to feel like home. I was keeping busy, had a sense of purpose, and enjoyed spending time with the new friends we had made over the last several months.

※

In early June I boxed up everything that wouldn't fit into our suitcases and shipped them back to a friend's house in Minneapolis.

The last meditation class was in mid-June. Arturo had the chairs set up and greeted me with a warm handshake before I started the class. "Hi everyone," I said, "practicing meditation with you for the last eleven months has been great. Shall we sit quietly together for the next twenty minutes?" I did my meditation practice at the same time the class was sitting in silence. Teaching meditation by talking can only take you so far. Sitting together in silence is the most effective way to pass on the meditative skills.

After the twenty minutes, I rubbed my hands together until they were warm, and opened my eyes into the warmth. The class joined me.

From the back, the botanist asked, "What about prayer?"

"Prayer?" I asked. In the previous eleven months it had never come up.

She nodded.

It took me a few seconds to respond. "There are things in life that can challenge us to our very core," I said. "Whether it is the death of a loved one, a diagnosis of a severe illness, or some other tragedy, sometimes life can drive you to your knees." I paused as I closed my eyes for a moment and tried to find my breath. "I don't know how I could get through those challenging times without it."

She nodded again, but still looked at me in anticipation.

"But you've heard me say many times that yoga is not a religion," I said. "Prayer is a very individual thing, so I can only speak for myself."

She and the others were staring intently at me.

"I can say that practicing meditation has helped me to understand and appreciate my own religion. Often at the end of my meditation practice, the urge for prayer arises naturally. At these times, I pray for the strength and wisdom to do what's right for myself and others. I also ask that the fruits of the meditation find their way to anyone in need." The lights blinked on and off as it started to rain. "When you get to that point, then you are doing the practice not for yourself, but for others, and it becomes very motivating to continue the practice."

At the end of class, Arturo came up to the front and presented me with a wooden plaque engraved with all the names of the students and the words, "Thank you from Panama."

Before everyone dispersed, I asked them to remain seated. "Is it OK if we end the class with one chanting of the word 'OM'?" Several in the class nodded and sat up in their chairs. OM is a sacred sound in Hinduism and Buddhism and a powerful mantra for chanting and meditation. Chanting it over and over again for a period of time can deepen a person's consciousness. The vibrations represent the universal sound. "Please use this as a breathing exercise, fully expanding at the rib cage on the inhalation." During the resounding chant, a flash of lightning lit up the room and was followed by a sharp, loud, crack of thunder.

The next day Arturo and I had lunch in the cafeteria near his office.

"It would be great if you can continue the classes here," I told him. I chewed on a piece of fried yucca root while he took a bite of his corn fritter.

"Will you come to Minneapolis later this summer for teacher training?" I asked.

"If I can find the money and get the time off," he said.

When I went to shake his hand after lunch, he brushed it aside and gave me a big hug.

Two days later I was back in Minneapolis, and Nikki returned two weeks after that.

CHAPTER TWO

Danny, Dan, Daniel

VULNERABLE — Practice the child's pose to feel safe and secure. (Sit in a kneeling position with the top of the feet on the floor, the buttocks resting on the heels, and the forehead resting on the floor. Rest the arms at the side with the palms upward.)

In June of 1969, I finished sixth grade. I was excited about leaving behind our small elementary school and moving on to a large junior high. The same group of my friends had been together since kindergarten. In seventh grade we would encounter a whole new group of classmates. Before that would happen, I had a few months of summer break.

"Do I have to go to Scout camp?" My dad and I were sitting at the kitchen table, ready for dinner. Tomahawk Scout Camp was in Birchwood, Wisconsin, over a two-hour drive from our house.

"What's wrong, Danny?" my mom asked. She set our plates of hamburger, tater tots, and peas on the table.

"I haven't learned all the stuff I'm supposed to know." I was nervous about being away from home without my parents for the first time. And I had never slept in a tent.

My mom looked expectantly at my dad. He had a quiet personality and a quirky sense of humor.

"I can help you with that," he offered. He had been in the same Scout troop thirty-five years before and used the knots when he was in the Merchant Marines in World War II.

The next night, my dad came home after work with the perfect piece of rope for tying knots. After dinner we sat on the couch together.

"You already know the square knot, right?" he asked.

I nodded.

"Here's how you do the bowline."

I tried it several times as he watched and corrected me.

"Attta boy," he said. "You practice on your own, and we'll do a different one tomorrow night."

We practiced the knots nightly for the next six weeks before I left for camp.

The week-long stay at Scout camp ended on July 20. The night I returned from camp, at 9:30 p.m., my mom, dad, and seventeen-year-old sister, Leslie, all gathered around the television. We watched with awe as Neil Armstrong walked on the moon! I ran outside and looked up at the clear half-moon, but I couldn't see the astronauts or their Apollo 11 spacecraft.

For the rest of the summer, I went back to my routine of playing ball with the neighborhood kids every chance we could. In the morning we played basketball in a driveway across the street, and in the afternoon we played baseball at the nearby school playground. If we needed an extra guy for the evening touch football game in our front yard, my gregarious, small-boned, left-handed mom would be the designated quarterback. She could throw farther than any of us.

On summer weekends we often spent the day at an outer-ring, suburban country club. The club was a thirty-minute drive from our three bedroom, rambler-style house on Rome Avenue in the Highland Park neighborhood of St. Paul. My dad played golf with his buddies, and my mom sunned by the pool with the other moms. I socialized with friends, played games in the pool, and ate at the snack bar.

During the last week of summer vacation before the start of seventh grade, I was in my bedroom, reorganizing how the clothes were arranged in my dresser.

My mom passed by. "Something changed about you at summer camp," she said. "You grew up."

☀

Nine months later, at the end of seventh grade, I had my Bar Mitzvah. It was the culmination of several years of after-school training in Hebrew. On Friday night I was supposed to sing the full version of the Kiddush, or blessing over the wine. This blessing was nine lines long with a total of forty-five Hebrew words. While I sat on the pulpit waiting for the cue for my part from the rabbi, I glanced around the full sanctuary of about two hundred people. In addition to the regular templegoers, all my friends were there, and more than a dozen relatives came from out of town for the event. My heart was racing in anticipation.

I stepped up to the podium and adjusted the microphone. When I started to sing the first line, my voice was shaky and out of sync with the organ player backstage. My parents were in the front row and had wide eyes and mouths open, hoping I would make it. The rabbi stared intently from the edge of his seat.

All the practice sessions I had done suddenly clicked into my brain, and I relaxed a little. On the second line, my rhythm settled into place, and my voice got strong and steady. The rabbi and my parents looked visibly relieved. I continued to belt out the moving melody and finished with my hand tapping on the podium and a big smile. The members of the audience joined me in smiling and nodded their heads in approval. Connecting with the large group of people and the ancient sounds of the Hebrew language was intoxicating.

During eighth grade, I went into the den one fall evening to turn on the TV. My fifty-one-year-old father was on the couch, reading the paper and smoking his usual cigar. "DJ, have a seat," he said. "I need to talk to you."

Right away I knew something was going on. He never asked me to sit down for a talk. My only sibling, Leslie, had already moved away to college.

"Your mom and I are having some trouble."

Nothing seemed different to me. I shrugged my shoulders. "Like what?"

"You know I love you," he said.

"Yes." I looked at him in anticipation.

"Your mom and I have talked it over."

There was something sad in his tone. Then it hit me what he was about to say.

"Sorry, but I think it is better that I move out," he said.

I started to cry. "You can't. That's not fair." I got up and ran to my room without letting him finish.

Several minutes later, my forty-three-year-old mom knocked on my bedroom door. "Can I come in?"

"OK," I said.

She sat on the side of the bed. "What your dad was trying to tell you is that when two people no longer get along, sometimes it's for the best that they separate."

I got so scared. More than anything else, I didn't want it to happen. "Please don't do it," I pleaded. Tears started flowing again.

She gave me a hug. "You know both of us love you very much."

I pulled away. "But why do it then?"

"It's a separation," she said. "We're not giving up yet."

That quieted me for a moment. A feeling of hope came to my mind.

"I'm sorry, this is hard on all of us," she said.

Word of the separation spread quickly among my friends and classmates. The divorce rate in the U.S. was climbing in 1971. Seeing counselors or family therapists was still not common, and I was never offered that option. It was excruciatingly painful to walk in the school halls and lunchroom for the first few days after the news got out. I was humiliated and knew the other students were talking about me. My posture slouched and I looked at the floor as I walked. Something inside of me shut down. Expressing my feelings to others became very difficult.

Two months later, they made the decision to get divorced.

My dad rented an apartment close to his wholesale men's accessory business in downtown St. Paul. Twice a week he would drive the twenty minutes to our house and take me out to dinner. Sometimes on the weekends I would go stay with him. I adjusted to the new routine quicker than I thought I would. My classmates soon forgot about my parents, and we all moved on to whatever the newest gossip was.

A year later, Mr. Hoff, my ninth-grade English teacher, stopped his lesson. "Hertz and Crane, out in the hall!" he yelled.

Crane and I sheepishly stood up and walked outside the room.

Mr. Hoff joined us after telling the class to read quietly. "Don't you think I can hear the two of you say my first name in class?" he asked.

Crane and I stood quietly.

"What was that?" he asked. "Why are you so quiet now?"

Both of us looked glum and remained silent.

He said, "I didn't choose my name, but I am proud of the name my parents gave me." He clenched his jaw and stared at us without blinking. "I expect both of you to show the proper respect. Do you understand?"

Both of us nodded. When I saw how hurt he was, I felt bad about what we had done.

"Go back in and finish the assignment."

The next day, in a school-wide ninth-grade assembly, Mr. Hoff was addressing the full auditorium of 500 students. All the core ninth-grade teachers patrolled the aisles to help keep everyone quiet. Mr. Hoff had information about the upcoming high school registration process on a large screen in the front of the auditorium. In 1972 St. Paul Highland Park High School didn't start until tenth grade, so as ninth-graders we were still in junior high.

Then, suddenly, from the row behind me, I could hear the name "Jack" yelled loudly. It echoed through the auditorium. Right away I recognized Crane's voice. I turned around, but Crane was already ducked down behind my seat. Mr. Hoff stopped speaking, looked up, and pointed towards the back of the auditorium. He spoke loudly into the microphone. "Hertz, wait outside!" The auditorium erupted in laughter as a teacher escorted me out.

After the assembly, Mr. Hoff met me at the auditorium door. "Dan, isn't it about time you grew up a little?"

I stood quietly.

"I expect more from you. As vice-president of the student council you are supposed to set an example for the other students."

"But this time it wasn't me," I said. "It came from behind me."

"Well, I'm talking to you right now."

"But I swear, it wa . . . "

Mr. Hoff cut me off. "Enough of the excuses. You just lost your Honors Pass. Hand it over."

I slowly took out the three-ring binder from my backpack, snapped it open, and sadly handed it over. The Honors Pass allowed me to go to anywhere in the school on my study periods in the modular schedule. Mod scheduling was started in the 1960s and was considered to be state of the art for junior high education at the time. There were sixteen twenty-four minute periods in each day that could be combined into shorter or longer classes.

I turned around to leave.

"Just a moment," he said.

I turned back. "Yes?"

"I hope someday you grow up to be a teacher and have a lot of students just like you."

In tenth grade, my first year of high school, I tried out for the swim team. Diving into a freezing cold pool at 6:30 a.m. after walking the half mile to school on a frigid winter morning was not fun. We were expected to be at practice for an hour every morning before school, two hours every day after school, and another two hours on Saturday morning. The chlorine dried up my skin and hair, and even with goggles, my eyes were red. Persevering through all the pain from the challenging workouts took a lot of discipline. Often I was tempted to quit.

The improvement in my times was just enough to encourage me to stick with it.

The punishing workouts continued to consume much of my time and energy in eleventh grade. Smooth rhythmic breathing and underwater silence became a way of life. That year a couple of friends got involved in drugs and drinking. I didn't like beer or smoking of any kind, so that held no interest for me. Even if it had, I would have been too tired from swim practice to join them.

A month before twelfth grade started, Richard Nixon resigned as president. During the school year, I finished my third year on the swim team and made plans to attend the University of Minnesota. Six weeks before our 1975 graduation ceremony, the Vietnam War officially ended.

The summer after graduation I got a job as a swim instructor.

On my first day of the summer job, a mom of one of the five-year-old non-swimmers pulled me aside. "My son did not want to come today."

I could see him hiding behind her, grabbing her legs.

The mom started to cry. "I don't know what to do. He is petrified of going near the water."

I bent down to talk to him. "It will be OK."

He started to cry too.

"How about if you two sit on the bench and just watch the class today?" I suggested.

They watched while the other students in the class had fun. After three days of watching, the kid finally trusted me enough to come in the water. He grabbed the side so hard I couldn't pry him off. He stayed in the water for a few minutes and then went back to sitting on the bench with his mom while I worked with the other students. This went on during daily lessons for two weeks.

During the third week, he let me slowly bring him around the pool while he tightly held onto me. By the fourth week, he relaxed enough to where he could stand up on his own, put his face in the water, blow bubbles, and kick. In the fifth week, he learned to float on his front and back. By the sixth and final week, he joined the rest of the class for the whole lesson. The kid learned all the skills necessary to move to the next level. I watched him paddle through the water with a great sense of satisfaction, knowing the connection between the two of us helped him overcome his fear.

✳

During my freshman year in college, I lived in a dormitory on campus. When it came time to declare a major, I had a strong interest in teaching. The feeling when that kid learned to swim was the most rewarding experience I ever had, and it stuck with me. But the job market in the area for teachers was terrible, and I decided to do something more practical. I chose to major in human resources management.

In May of freshman year, my mom called. "I'm selling the house."

"Why?" I asked.

"It is too much to take care of by myself, and I don't need such a big place."

"I'll need a place to stay for part of the summer," I said.

"You can stay in the second bedroom of my new apartment whenever you need to."

Later on that same day, my dad called. Since the divorce five years before we continued to see each other a couple of times a week. Neither of my parents had remarried.

"Now that your grandma is gone, there is no need for me to stay in town," he said. My dad's mom passed away in the nursing home a few months before.

I'm here, what about me? "But what about your business? What will you do?" I asked. He had run the business for over thirty years, since 1944.

"I'm selling the business. I have something set up with my brothers in Dallas."

The calls from my mom and dad shook me up. Ready or not, I was now an adult. Everything was changing—very suddenly. The earth felt like it was crumbling beneath my feet in the same way it did in eighth grade when they told me they were separating. It was strange that they both called on the same day. I guess they were still a little in-sync, even after living apart for five years.

I went for a longer run than usual that day as if I was trying to run away from the news they gave me. Finals week was coming up, and I buried myself in my studies. I just kept going and didn't talk to anyone about it.

After graduating from college at the age of twenty-two, I decided I wanted to be an actor. So much for my practical decision of majoring in human resources management. Ever since my Bar Mitzvah I wanted to be in a play, but in high school, swim practice always got in the way. Now I wanted to do it more than anything.

I got a day job working in hospital supply and went to a few crowded auditions in Minneapolis and St. Paul, with no success. At an audition in an outer-ring suburb, about twenty miles away, the stage manager signed me in and gave me a script to read. I gave her my resume and picture. When my name was called in the lobby, I walked out onto the small stage.

I shielded my eyes from the bright lights. A voice came from the seats.

"Welcome. I'm the director," he said in a British accent. "To my right is the assistant director, and to my left is the playwright. He is from the local community here." As my eyes adjusted I got a glimpse of them. They looked nice enough.

"You are Daniel?" he asked.

"Yes."

"Great! It says here on your resume that you recently graduated from college and you are an Eagle Scout."

I nodded.

"That's all very impressive, but have you had any acting classes, Daniel?" he asked.

"No."

"Any acting experience?"

"Well, yes, I listed it on the resume," I said.

There was a pause and I squinted at him through the lights. I could see he was reading my information.

"The only thing I see here is singing the Kiddush at your Bar Mitzvah," he said.

"That's correct," I replied.

He cast me in my first play. The part was a decent-sized supporting role as an astronaut in a science fiction play. It was the only time that the locally written play was ever produced. I learned all the theatre lingo such as stage left, stage right, blocking, and tech week.

One year after I graduated from college, the grind of the hospital job and the many audition rejections that had to be endured between parts started to wear me down. Having a meaningful day job became the most important thing for me. I went back to school and got my grades one through six teaching license. My experience teaching swimming showed me that with the right teacher, anyone could learn. A teacher made all the difference in the world. The Twin Cities area job market for elementary teachers was still very tight, but my mind was made up to go anywhere it took to get a job.

CHAPTER THREE

A New Teacher

STEADINESS — Practice the mountain pose to maintain steadiness in the face of an overwhelming challenge. (Stand firmly upright, yet relaxed, with the feet six to twelve inches apart. Unlock the knees. Relax the arms and hands at the side of the body.)

Two minutes into my first lesson as a brand new teacher, the sixth-grader in the front row yelled, "Shut up you white honkey motherfucker." There was never a case like this in any of my education textbooks. In a split second I had to decide on how I would respond. There were a few scattered chuckles from the other students, but they mostly looked wide-eyed at me in anticipation of whatever would happen next. It was showtime for them.

"Move to the desk in the corner of the classroom!" The previous Friday I had placed the desk there for timeouts. The student stood up like he was going to move, then hesitated and remained standing at his desk. I could tell he wanted to save face in front of the other students. And so did I.

"What is your name?" I asked sternly.

He grudgingly answered, "Xavier."

Because of my memorization work over the weekend, I responded with his last name. "Johnson?" This was enough to give him pause and throw him off a bit. Our eyes met for a second and he could see that I was fighting mad. Xavier didn't know what I would do next. He went, as instructed, but made a few comments under his breath along the way.

Two months before, I had finished my teacher education program. Two weeks before, I received a job offer from Dallas Independent School District (DISD) to teach sixth grade for an annual salary of fifteen thousand dollars. Two days before my required start date for the 1982–83 school year, I arrived at my new apartment in north Dallas.

My little 1980 Honda Civic hatchback was big enough to hold everything I owned: a folding card table, two folding chairs, a single-size futon mattress, and a duffel bag full of clothes. I was twenty-four years old and moving out of the state of Minnesota for the first time. A single highway—Interstate 35—spanned the one thousand miles from Minneapolis to Dallas. Halfway to my destination, I stopped at a motel in Kansas City for the night. My watch alarm was set to go off every hour because I was worried about the car sitting in the motel lot all night full of everything I owned. Every time the alarm went off, I would pop up in bed, take a look at my car out the window, and try to go back to sleep. In addition to worrying about my things in the car, I was thinking about my new job.

The morning after the first, restless night in my new apartment, I called the school and made an appointment to meet my new principal, Mr. Walters. It was a Thursday, and the students were scheduled to start the following Tuesday, after Labor Day. When I interviewed for the job earlier that summer, it was at the district headquarters. I never saw the school or met the principal. At the time, DISD was the seventh largest school district in the country, and they had a teacher shortage. They hired a lot of teachers from northern states such as Michigan and Minnesota. I ended up interviewing with

Dallas because I was in town to visit my dad who was living in the area at the time.

On a map, the school looked like it was about twenty miles south of where my apartment was located. It was a hot and steamy ninety-six degrees outside, which was average for Dallas in August. Without AC in my car, I sweated the whole way. I must have had the only car without AC since I didn't see anyone else on the highway with the windows open. As I clicked on the car radio, the announcer said he was about to introduce a brand new song from a new recording artist from Minneapolis—"Little Red Corvette" by Prince.

I pulled up to the front of the school. It started to sink in that this was where I would be driving five days a week for the next nine months. The three story, nondescript, rectangular school building looked like it was built in the 1950s. Many windows were open, with no AC in sight. The neighborhood around the school was made up of small, single-family, rambler-style homes from around the same era as the school. The homes looked similar to the ones from the neighborhood where I grew up. I entered the building, and a short left through bare halls got me to the office.

The principal met me at the office door. He was a large, heavy-set, gray haired African American with thick glasses. His slightly worn dark suit and tie seemed overly formal to wear on such a hot day, especially considering the students and teachers had not yet started. I wore my usual cotton button-down shirt and a pair of khakis. He looked tired, but carried himself upright with a solemn dignity. We shook hands and I could feel the strength of his grip.

He said, "Good morning, Mr. Hertz." His expression never changed.

I smiled. "How are you today?"

He didn't respond, only pointed me in the direction of a small conference room. After we were seated and facing each other, he paused to look me over. His expression turned to a frown as he took off his glasses and rubbed his eyes.

He put his glasses back on. "I have been thinking about this for a long time. It is best you send the students to me, rather than hit them," he said.

I smiled a little, and when it wasn't returned, my smile turned into a confused frown.

He stood up. "Is there anything else?" he asked.

"What subject will I be teaching?"

He shook my hand. "You'll get your teaching and room assignment first thing tomorrow morning, the same as everybody else."

I headed back to my car. *Could he be serious?* Corporal punishment was already illegal in Minnesota.

The next day came and went quickly. I got my class rosters, met a few of my colleagues, and collected textbooks and supplies. The other teachers were very busy, but they did their best to say hello and introduce themselves. Most of the teachers were older African American women from the neighborhood, and a few were like me—younger white teachers from the north. Finally, toward the end of the day, I caught up with Mrs. Portis, one of the fifth-grade teachers. She was from the neighborhood and had been at the school a long time. I showed her my class roster.

"Oh, Lordy, you're gonna need the Lordy to get through this year." Then she laughed and whistled through her teeth. "Honey, you poor thing," she said. "You look like a sweet young man. Where are you from?"

"Minnesota."

"You've come a long way to join us. I have another meeting to get to but wish you luck. Stop by anytime." She smiled and went on her way.

There was only about an hour left in the prep day. I had already made alphabetical seating charts, put names on the assigned desks, and threw up some bulletin boards that I made while student teaching. It was slowly sinking in that this was my classroom.

The last thing I had time to do before heading home was to make a poster with the class rules and expectations:

- When the teacher is talking, listen quietly
- Follow directions
- Raise your hand if you want to speak or leave your seat
- Keep your hands, feet, and objects to yourself

Over the three-day weekend, I worked on my lesson plans for the week. The K–8 school had an enrollment of 800 students. My schedule would be teaching ninety minutes of sixth-grade language arts and ninety minutes of sixth-grade social studies every day to two different sections. There were twenty-four students assigned to each section. I also spent time that weekend memorizing the names of the students. While student teaching, I discovered that if I memorized the student names ahead of time, it was an instant way to build rapport. By doing this, when a student said their first name, I could say their last name.

As I drove into work on the first day of school, I tried to rehearse what I would say, but my mind was jumping all over the place. The lesson plans and the student names got all jumbled up. In the morning heat of the busy highway, I was sweating more than usual.

Standing outside the classroom door, I greeted the students as they entered the room. "Please find your name on the assigned desk and have a seat." As I looked around and saw the students walk through the halls and enter the classrooms, it was clear that every student in the school was African American.

I knew that as a public school teacher, I would be working with whoever walked in the door and that it would most likely be a diverse group. Even so, I was surprised that such a place existed. For several years, the schools in Minneapolis had been busing students all over the city to integrate the schools. But the way Minneapolis integrated their schools was not going to change the facts of this situation. I was a new white teacher with a lot to learn, and all the students were black. We would be spending many hours together over the next nine months.

The bell rang, everyone was seated in their assigned seats, and I began class by going over the rules. "When I am talking, no one else is talking. Is that clear?" *So far so good.* Being very strict and serious was what I was advised to do on the first day by my education professors and other teachers. Then, before I could get the next sentence out, Xavier yelled the obscenity at me from the front row.

At the end of that first day, one of the students stopped in the classroom on his way home. "Mr. Hertz, why don't you whup these kids when they are talking out of turn?"

"Thanks for the suggestion, Curtis, but that is not gonna work for me."

He slowly shook his head and looked amused as he walked out the door.

Most of the older, black women teachers from the neighborhood used corporal punishment in their classrooms. They didn't hesitate to hit the students when they misbehaved. The math teacher across the hall had four wooden rulers taped together and whacked the students on their thighs if they got out of line. I could hear the crack of the rulers now and then throughout the day. The science teacher down the hall had a plastic whiffle ball bat. She would bring the problem student out in the hall and have them bend over. The sound would reverberate down the hall.

Often the lessons I developed in the beginning of the year would erupt in noise, especially if they required more abstract thinking and some reading on their own. I found this out when introducing my first social studies lesson.

"Please open your book to page five and read the section on the Battle of Bunker Hill. In five minutes we'll discuss why this was such a key battle in the Revolutionary War."

I glanced around the room. "Let's go, two minutes have passed and, Jamar, you don't even have your book out."

"I don't have my book," he responded.

"That is not going to help you learn. Slide over and share with Marquis."

"He stinks. I don't want to share with him." The class laughed.

Marquis knew better than to respond. Jamar would have socked him in the eye.

I moved on to the next issue. "Melvin, your book is open, but it is upside down and on the wrong page." I went over to help him find the correct page.

"Don't touch my book," he said quietly.

Larena said loudly, "I can't read with all this noise."

"Too bad," shouted Antoine from across the room.

Larena shouted back at him. "Shut up or I'll make you shut up."

Antoine stood up. "Let's go, right now."

Larena never backed down to anybody. She moved toward Antoine. He was bigger than she was, but he knew she was tougher. The other students were cheering and egging them on.

I stepped in the middle. "Enough. Sit down!"

They continued threatening each other as they inched closer. I had to get Antoine out of there or he would get hurt.

"Antoine," I shouted. "Let's go. Out in the hall, now!" He didn't move.

Then I heard Curtis, a cheerful, well-liked student, quietly whisper to Antoine. "It isn't worth it."

This was enough for Antoine to pause. He was looking for an out. I guided him outside as quickly as I could.

"Wait out here for the office referral." I wrote the referral, kept an eye on the class, and handed it out the door to Antoine. Larena, Curtis, and Nia were the only ones still reading. Jamar shot spitballs across the room, Marquis made a paper airplane, and Xavier was out of his desk, running around the room.

After school that day I went to visit the special education teacher down the hall.

"What can you tell me about Melvin?" I asked.

She got a folder out of the file cabinet and handed it to me.

"He can't read a lick," she said.

I looked over his assignments in the folder. He was still working on writing the letters of the alphabet.

"Know anything about his family?" I asked

"We've tried to get them in here for his IEP meeting but no response," she said.

"Thanks," I said.

A huge issue was that DISD required the students to use the sixth-grade-level social studies books and would not allow the students to use easier books that they could actually read. That is how DISD thought you bring the students up to grade level, rather than starting at the level they were at and gradually increasing the difficulty. This was a recipe for disaster. Some of the students had the skills for any assignment I gave them, but others didn't know how to read beyond the first-grade level.

On top of the academic frustration, the principal did not want the students taking a recess break, and they did not have a physical education class every day. I talked to the principal about this early on when he was passing by my room.

"Mr. Walters, I think recess would really be a healthy way for the students to work off the extra energy."

"Recess is for little kids," he said. "I don't want them getting into trouble on the playground." Then he walked away.

If I wanted to finish a more complicated lesson, I had to yell over the noise to anyone who wanted to listen. Often during that first month I went home with a sore throat from all the yelling. The stress of the job took a toll on me. While looking in the bathroom mirror one morning before school, I pulled my hair back and clearly noticed the hairline was receding.

When I was away from school at night or on the weekends, it was like wearing a coat of stress that I could not take off. I became friends with a couple of the younger teachers on the staff who had also been recruited from up north to come to the school. We would occasionally go out after work. The conversation would inevitably turn to how challenging the students were. This only served to further stress me out.

The only strategy I had for dealing with the stress was to exercise regularly. That had worked for me for years, but it was not enough to help during this time. I couldn't let go of that feeling of unease. Quitting probably would have been the easiest thing to do, but for me it was never an option that I considered. I moved across the country and invested a lot of time and money in getting my teacher licensure. This was my first "real" job, and I had too much pride to walk away.

The school didn't have a staff lounge. We were required to eat in the student lunchroom, but at least all the teachers could sit at a separate table. That was far from relaxing. Listening to the teachers complain about their students was like fingernails being scraped on the chalkboard.

The joy and enthusiasm I had for teaching and life when I arrived in Dallas six weeks before were slowly seeping out of me. When Sunday night came around, my mood would change to sadness, knowing I would have to face the students again the next day. My plans to return to Minneapolis on Thanksgiving and winter break gave me something to look forward to.

Behavior management continued to be the biggest challenge. The first thing I had to do was figure out a way to improve the classroom management, otherwise we would never be able to do anything. By mid-October, I settled on simpler assignments that didn't require a lot of explanation. The class got quiet during spelling tests, so we had a pre- and post-test each week. They were also very quiet when they were copying word definitions from the dictionary. The quiet classroom was a relief, but this type of rote learning would have upset the professors in the education classes I took the year before. Rote learning did not show the students how to understand or apply what they were copying down. Nevertheless, the students were used to doing this type of busywork in previous years, and it was soothing for them.

When a student misbehaved, one choice I had was to send them to the office, as the principal requested in our initial meeting. But it wasn't really a great choice. They would come back so sore they couldn't sit down.

When I was tired or not feeling well and my patience had run out, all I wanted to do was teach a quiet lesson without any disruption. The thought of hitting the students crossed my mind. I was in an environment where it was normal and accepted, and the teachers that used it had quiet classrooms. But in the end, it felt too foreign. I had never been hit in my life, at home or school. Even the thought of it was too hurtful, and I was able to resist the temptation. Hitting the students was a short term solution that allowed the staff to survive each day, but it was also teaching the students that violence was the way to solve problems. When the principal was in the vicinity, the students behaved out of fear. If the students found out he left the building, behavior issues would pop-up all over the school.

In late October, I set up some positive reinforcements for the students. Each row that quieted down when I started to teach would get a point. At the end of the day, I would give the students in the row with the highest points a positive letter to take home:

Dear (name of parent or guardian),

Your child did a great job in school today. Thank you for your support.

Sincerely,
Mr. Daniel Hertz
6th Grade Teacher

The letter helped a little with the behavior. I had other ideas, but what the principal expected of me was to fit into a very narrow range of teaching styles and strategies. He did not like cooperative learning, where the students worked in groups. That was the preferred method of instruction that was taught at the time at the University of Minnesota, College of Education. With cooperative learning, the higher-level students could have helped the lower-level ones. Mr. Walters wanted the students in rows, working quietly.

Every day after lunch I read to the students. One day Mr. Walters walked into the room and saw me doing this. The whole class was sitting quietly and listening. Even so, at the end of school that day, he came into my room. "Mr. Hertz, reading to the students is for little kids, not sixth-graders." It wasn't a discussion. He left the room after that one sentence, before I could respond. I continued to read to the students after lunch, and I knew that he knew about it, but he never mentioned it again.

At the end of October, I wrote this writing prompt on the board, "If I had a million dollars, I would . . . " and found out that a lot of the students liked to write. As soon as they saw the prompt, most of them got out a paper and pencil and started on the assignment. Some could only write a simple sentence, and others could write a paragraph. Curtis wrote, "I would buy my momma a big, new house." Marquis wrote, "I would buy the best Nike Air Force 1 basketball shoes in the whole school." Jamar wrote, "I would buy me this school and get some fun classes." Each week after that I gave them a writing prompt. They had to revise it during the week after I made some corrections. At the end of each week, I put the best writing on the bulletin board. They loved it if what they wrote got posted on the board for everyone to see.

In mid-November, a woman from the district office came to observe my class and loved the student writing samples that she saw on the bulletin board.

The principal called me down to the office at the end of the day. He sat behind his desk. Hanging on the wall behind him was the paddle he used on the students.

"Mr. Hertz, I don't know what you said to those big shots from downtown, but they mentioned you in their report."

"In a good way?" I sat up in my chair.

"Somehow you charmed them. We have a lot of good teachers here who have never gotten a mention from any visitor."

"OK." I slouched, sat in silence, and waited.

"That's all," he concluded.

I left the room.

Even though Mr. Walters wasn't impressed, the feedback from the district office inspired me, and I continued to offer weekly writing prompts. In the beginning of December, I wrote this on the chalkboard: "Who is your favorite musician and why?" The students started shouting the name of the musician before they even got out a piece of paper.

Antoine yelled, "Billie Jean is not my lover."

The class laughed.

Every single student said Michael Jackson. That was no surprise. He had just released his *Thriller* album. The sales were off the charts, and it was on pace to become the biggest selling album of all time.

The best day of the year for me was December 17, the last day of school before winter break. My excitement for the two week vacation was exhilarating.

☀

Even though returning to Dallas after two weeks in Minneapolis was psychologically devastating, I had another idea I wanted to try. The Sunday night before the first day back from winter break, I made some calls to the parents of my students.

"Mrs. Morton, this is Daniel Hertz, Marquis's teacher."

"Yes."

"It is nice to speak to you," I said. "I have enjoyed working with Marquis this year."

"Thank you for calling. Happy New Year to you," she said. "Can I help you?"

"Mostly I wanted to introduce myself and let you know I plan to call regularly from now on."

"That is very nice of you."

"Please encourage Marquis to get off to a good start tomorrow."

"I sure will. Good night."

I continued to make calls that night and spent at least an hour every night calling when students did well or when they misbehaved. Spending the time was no problem for me because I found something that worked. Each day I kept a list of students who did things well and also those who misbehaved. The students learned that when I said I would call their home, I did. It took a few calls, but eventually their parents, or whoever they lived with, started to like and trust me. The students wanted to get a good phone call because if they did, something good would usually happen at home. On the other hand, if I made a negative phone call about some problem that day, there would be a punishment given at home. Often it meant a whipping for the student with what they called a switch.

One of the more mischievous students lived with his grandmother. When I called her one time, she confided in me, "Mr. Hertz, I'm an old lady. I appreciate all your calls. I know how much trouble Antoine can be. I'm doing my best, but I'm not strong enough to whip him."

"Mrs. Smith, I appreciate your support. Whatever you can do will be helpful. The main thing is that he knows we are in touch. I am really concerned he is not taking his studies seriously."

She replied, "Don't you worry. I have a plan."

The next day, Antoine came to school and was very angry with me. "Did you tell my grandma to whup me in my sleep?"

"I talked to her, but I don't know anything about that."

"Don't call her again," he responded.

"Sit down and do your work and I won't have to."

At the end of the day, I told Antoine, "You did a good job today. Here is a positive letter to give to your grandma." He nodded and took the letter as he left the room.

For a couple of the students who didn't have phones, I made in-person home visits and sent notes home. In January, one family invited me over for dinner. I was so happy when Nia handed me the invitation from her father. It re-ignited some of the enthusiasm for teaching I had felt only a few months before. To sit down to dinner with a family had the potential to build the trust and positive relationship that was necessary for the student's academic progress.

Their home was very close to the school. The father was a disabled vet in a wheelchair and the mother did the cooking. We ate shortly after I arrived. They went to a lot of trouble to make a really nice, traditional southern meal. The pan-fried chicken, mashed potatoes, black-eyed peas, and collard greens tasted great. Nia, the student, was thrilled to have me over. She had a couple of younger siblings.

Her younger brother asked me, "Are you rich?"

I smiled but didn't answer. I was still sleeping on a futon on the floor and using the folding chairs I had hauled down in my little Honda Civic.

He asked, "What kind of car do you have?"

Before I could answer he was hushed by his parents.

Two weeks after the dinner at Nia's house, something happened in school that upset her family. Nia was a small, sweet girl who did all the assignments. But one day, she lost her temper and cussed at one of the other students. I had to send her to the office for her own safety and to settle the class down.

An hour later she returned to the class. She was paddled in the office and came back very sullen and quiet, with tears in her eyes.

That night I called her home and her dad answered. "Hi, Mr. Cromwell, sorry to report that I had to send Nia to the office today. She cussed at another student in the middle of our spelling lesson. It was very disruptive to the class."

"I am sorry to hear that," he said. "It won't happen again."

"Good, thank you," I said. "There is one other thing. She was paddled down in the office and was crying when she came back to the room."

"Damn, that is not right," he said.

I didn't say anything, just waited for him to continue.

"We do not want our little girl hit by anyone in that school. I'll talk to Nia, but please do not send her to that office again."

"Yes sir, I understand. I am sorry it happened and will do everything I can to prevent it in the future."

Since the class behavior was improving a little, in February I arranged for the local state representative from the Texas legislature to visit the social studies class. He was an African American man who was well known in the local neighborhood. My goal was to teach the students the importance of getting involved politically if they thought that something was unfair. It was very difficult to get a response from the representative's office. I had called his office a couple of times a week since winter break. His assistant would always say they were working on it, and that he would come by as soon as he could. Finally, after much persistence, a time was set up for the visit.

Without me asking, some of the students dressed up in their Sunday best for the visitor. As soon as the car pulled up to the school, they all rushed to the window to see him. I thought, *Oh no, this isn't going well.* Before I could tell them to get away from the window and sit down, they straightened the rows, picked up any trash on the floor, and sat up in their desks. I was amazed to observe it all. They listened quietly to the speaker and asked the questions that we had spent a lot of time preparing.

At the end of the day, Mr. Walters came to see me.

He asked, "How did you get the representative to show up? We have tried to get him for a school assembly many times."

"His office secretary must have gotten tired of hearing from me."

"Well, next time let me know, would you? I could have arranged an assembly for the whole school."

My smile from the success of the lesson turned into disappointment at his reaction. I never even knew the school had assemblies. Regardless of what he thought, it showed me that bringing in relevant role models from the community could really help these students. Pursuing it any further that year seemed fruitless since no one else in the school was bringing in speakers, and DISD had no system for screening guest speakers.

I continued with the daily phone calls. Most of the students' behavior improved dramatically by the end of February. By this time, I had adjusted to the make-up of the student body, living in the south for the first time, and working in a community with very limited resources. The schools in Dallas were funded by local property taxes, which meant that the wealthier neighborhoods in the northern part of the city got more money. This system perpetuated the haves and have-nots.

By March, the students and I learned to trust each other and became much more at ease with each other. Even my relationship with Xavier improved. We moved on from the obscenity he said the first day of school. Before school one day, he brought his younger brother by the room.

"This is Mr. Hertz, the guy I have been talking about all the time," he said. "Someday he might be your teacher."

His brother smiled shyly.

"Keep doing your homework every day, and maybe we'll see you in a few years," I said.

My confidence grew, and I taught with more conviction. The behavior patterns of the students and the skills they were lacking became clear to me. Larena, the student who almost got into the fight with Antoine in the beginning of the year, came in after school one day and asked me to help her with the upcoming speech contest. She had taken the initiative to memorize a beautiful speech. We rehearsed after school for several days, and she did a great job in the contest. When I saw her on stage, competing with the other top students in the school, I was so proud of her. The experience with Larena helped me to once again see each student in that sixth-grade class in the same way I had seen the five-year-old non-swimmer from six years before. That kid in the pool transformed so much in a few weeks, and I knew it was possible for these students too.

Even though things were clearly going better, there were various ongoing behavior issues. These were challenging students whose behavior couldn't be changed overnight. Most of the families cared a lot about how the students were doing. For the few I could not contact, I had to continue sending those students to the office when they misbehaved.

In April, after spring break, I was driving home from school and saw Melvin walking on a side road in the neighborhood. He was the special education student who couldn't read, and no matter what I tried, I could not reach him or his family. I stopped the car and got out. *Maybe if I talked to him away from school, it would be different.* He saw me coming, picked up an empty liquor bottle that was near him on the ground, broke it on a rock, and waved it at me. I quickly returned to my car and headed home.

At the end of April, Mr. Walters stepped in the room to see how the class was going. The rows were lined up, the students were quiet, and I was up front teaching a lesson.

"Row 1 gets a point." I marked it on the chalkboard. "Row 2, row 3, row 4, row 5, and row 6 are all sitting quietly. Every row gets a point."

They watched me mark the slashes on the chalkboard.

"OK, time for the weekly contest. We have been studying these history questions all week. Same rules as usual. Your row gets a point if someone in your row gets the correct answer." They all waited quietly. "Row 1, who can name three of the original colonies?"

We continued in an orderly manner. For the first time ever, I saw a faint smile on the principal's face. Then something caught his eye. He looked directly at Jamar, in the back corner, and calmly said, "Throw out your gum, son." Then he walked out the door. Everyone in the room turned to look at Jamar. He was still chewing the gum.

"Jamar, if I were you, I would throw out the gum," I told him.

He shook his head, said, "Muh, muh," and continued to chew away, harder than ever. He wanted to make sure all the students could see he was not scared.

I continued with the lesson. About five minutes later, the principal opened the door and peeked in the room. He looked at Jamar to see if he was still chewing. Without saying a word, he walked quickly into the room, and in one smooth move yanked off his long leather belt. The students and I stared with open mouths and big eyes. I had never seen anything like that, and the students also looked shocked. Before I could take it all in, he marched to Jamar, grabbed him by the arm, and effortlessly pulled him out of his desk. He aimed for Jamar's buttocks as he whipped him with the belt, but Jamar was squirming all over, and the blows from the belt landed across his back.

Jamar started crying and screaming. "I'm gonna tell my mama. I'm gonna tell my mama."

The principal told him in his booming, preacher-like voice, "Go ahead, I've been wanting to talk to her for a long time."

After the principal left, Jamar sat back down and buried his head in his arms.

"Sorry, Jamar," I said.

He responded with a muffled, "You shut up."

We went back to the weekly contest. No one in the room looked at him or even smiled. We all knew it was no time to rub salt in the wound.

After school one day in May, Curtis stopped by the room. He asked, "Can you help me with this math assignment?"

Even though I wasn't teaching math that year, I gave it a shot. "Let's have a look, Mr. Curtis." I smiled and said, "We can do this."

He relaxed, nodded, and smiled back.

"Take the chalk and show me how you would work out the first problem."

When he was finished, I said, "You set the fractions up correctly. But when you divide fractions, you change the division sign to a multiplication sign and flip over the second fraction." He tried it again and did it correctly. "That's right. Nice work."

"That was cool, thank you," he said. "You should be a math teacher."

I took what Curtis said to heart. Teaching math was fun. If

someone couldn't read well, at least there was a chance they could still do the calculations. Math problems had only one answer. In social studies, the answer wasn't always so clear.

Three weeks before the end of the school year, as I sat down for lunch with the other teachers, I overhead Mrs. Portis, the fifth-grade teacher, talking to another colleague. "I can't believe he has lasted the year. They put all the bad ones in the same classroom."

I didn't say anything. When she saw me, she dropped the subject. It was disappointing. Placing all the most behavior-challenged students in the same class was a setup for failure before I even walked in the room.

Later that same day, I ran into Mrs. Portis in the hallway. She told me, "Congratulations on making it this far. Many others before you who had been recruited from the north left before they finished the year. I know how tough it was, but you made it and did a good job."

I smiled. "Thanks for the encouragement. It helps to know that."

On the last day of school, I said goodbye to the students and didn't mention my plans for the next school year. A few gave a quick wave on their way out of the room. They were so excited to leave, they almost trampled each other.

After school on that last day, I played in a pick-up basketball game with some students and staff. This was the only time all year that they organized something like that. We high-fived and hollered with joy after each score. I finally started to feel at home in that culture and school. Things improved over the course of the year, and I was sure it would have gone much better the next year. Even given all that, the decision to leave was easy. I had visited Austin, Texas, on my spring break and loved the lakes, walking paths, and the big university. It reminded me a lot of Minneapolis. My plan for the following year was to work for the school district in Austin and study for my secondary math license at night.

The euphoria of being done with my job in Dallas allowed me to drive the twenty hours back to Minneapolis without stopping for the night.

CHAPTER FOUR

Goodbye to Mom

GRIEF — Practice the corpse pose for deep healing and rejuvenation. (Lie on your back with eyes closed. Place feet a comfortable distance apart. Place arms away from the side of the body with palms up.)

After three years of teaching in Texas, I moved back to Minneapolis in the summer of 1985. Shortly after moving back, I had an interview for a junior high math teacher position with the Minneapolis Public Schools. While in Texas, I finished my secondary math licensure, and it transferred back to Minnesota. During the interview, I told the principal of Franklin Jr. High about my experience in Dallas. At the end of the interview, she offered me the job. My new principal was an African American woman about forty years old.

"I'm assigning you to be the math teacher for a brand new program for eighth-grade students," she said. All of the students would be in eighth grade for the second year in a row. Retained students are considered at-risk for dropping out.

"They are prime candidates for joining gangs and getting involved with drugs," she said.

"Sounds like a challenge, that's for sure," I replied.

"It will be."

She went on to explain that I would be teamed with an English teacher and a behavior specialist for fifteen to twenty students. The team would have complete control over how the day was managed, independent of the rest of the school. The assistant principal would support the team.

Minneapolis Public Schools was on the forefront of a national movement that retained students in kindergarten, fourth, and eighth grades who couldn't pass a Benchmark Basic Skills Test. The Minneapolis superintendent at the time was Dr. Richard Green. Benchmark testing was his signature policy, so the program was well funded.

Two weeks into the school year, the behavior specialist on our team was teaching a lesson on time management skills to the twenty students in the retention class.

A student named Larry interrupted her. He shouted, "This is stupid. I had all this stuff last year!"

She stopped teaching and spoke in a neutral, matter-of-fact tone. "One-one-thousand, two-one-thousand, three-one thousand." She continued to count until Larry quieted down. When he was quiet, she said, "Thank you for your attention in three seconds." Without raising her voice, she continued teaching.

I couldn't believe the technique she used was working. Her facial expression never changed. *What would the students in Dallas think of this lady?* Often during my year of teaching in Dallas, I responded to an angry student with an even angrier tone. This escalated the situation. The experience of team teaching in the retention program showed me that every teacher developed their own classroom management style. One teacher could be authoritative, another could be democratic. Both could be very effective.

Two minutes later, Larry shouted again. "Why don't you answer my question?"

She continued with her lesson and ignored him.

Learning to ignore a student who was misbehaving was one of the hardest things for me to learn. Winning or losing an argument was not the point. The main question was whether the behavioral goal was reached or not.

Another two minutes passed. Larry stood up and pushed his desk over. He yelled, "This is stupid! Why doesn't anyone listen to me?"

I stood in the back of the room, waiting for a signal from the behavior specialist on how I could help. Team teaching in the same room took a while to get used to. Do you jump in and assist and look like you are taking over, or do you hang back and wait for instructions from the main teacher?

The teacher remained calm. "You have five seconds to pick up the desk, sit down, and get back to work."

Five seconds passed and Larry stood there with his arms folded over his chest.

The teacher said, "You have made the choice to take a time out in the back room."

As Larry walked slowly toward the timeout room, he said, "You have three seconds to leave me alone."

The class laughed.

The teacher ignored it.

He made it to the back room, and she continued the lesson.

If Larry had refused to go to the back room, he would have been sent across the hall to see the assistant principal. In Dallas that meant the student would most likely be paddled. Here they could be suspended from school. Suspending the students was not desirable since the biggest problem we had was truancy. Larry had already missed four out of the first ten days of school. If a student showed up, we were confident we could teach them.

Two months into the school year, I applied for and received a five-hundred-dollar grant to start a cross-age tutoring program with a nearby elementary school. The grant money would be used to pay for buses so both classes could go together on field trips to the neighborhood and downtown libraries. The principals of both schools gave their approval, and I found a second-grade teacher who volunteered to participate. When I told the eighth-graders about the program, I made it clear that they could only participate if they attended regularly and behaved appropriately while visiting the other school.

For the first two weeks of the project, twice a week we blocked out ninety minutes in the schedule. We walked with the eighth-graders over to the elementary school. Our plan was to use the grant money for field trips later on, after the students got to know their cross-age buddy. The first meeting was an introductory activity in the second-grade classroom. Before walking over for the second visit, we role modeled and prepped the students on how to read a picture book to a younger kid. The second meeting was held in the elementary school library.

Larry saw his second-grade buddy on the other side of the library, sulking in a corner. He walked over to him and squatted down. "What's going on with you today, little buddy?"

"I don't like to read. I hate school."

"I hate school too," Larry said. "All you have to do is pick out any book in the library that looks good, and I'll read it to you." Larry held out his hand and helped his buddy stand up. Together they found a book and a quiet spot in the corner. Larry started to read to him.

On the way back to Franklin, I caught up to Larry and talked to him as we walked. "You did a great job with that second-grader. Where did you learn to work so well with little kids?"

"I have a little brother," Larry said.

"Well, you did a great job," I said. "Keep it up!"

He nodded and gave me the beginning of a small smile before walking ahead of me.

At Franklin we had a significant amount of success with about 80 percent of the students passing the Benchmark Test the second time around. In Larry's case, his attendance improved enough for him to pass the tests. Working with these students showed me once again that everyone was capable of learning if you could figure out what was blocking their progress.

But the test scores didn't improve for everyone, and it led to very large class sizes around the district. Kindergarten teachers couldn't fit all the students they had in their rooms. There were seven- and eight-year-olds in the same room as five-year-olds. The question remained: What do you do with students who repeat the same grade three years in a row?

Dr. Green was hired as chancellor of the New York City Public Schools, the largest public school system in the country. The retention program in Minneapolis was discontinued.

❋

After my third year at Franklin, I fully realized the importance of having a summer break after each grueling school year. Even though I liked my job and found it fulfilling, by the end of each year my level of patience became shorter and shorter. Like social workers and nurses, teaching is a very giving profession. I desperately needed that time in the summer to relax and recover.

At the end of my fourth year at Franklin, I applied for a job as a district-wide mentor teacher and was shocked to learn I got it after a relatively short time in the district. Teachers being released from part of their day to mentor new teachers was a brand new concept. The Minneapolis Teachers' Union contract was on the cutting edge of a national movement to empower teachers to help other teachers.

❋

On June 6, 1990, the last day of my first year as a mentor teacher, I got an unexpected call from my mother. Her pulse raced to one hundred fifty beats per minute during an annual physical. She asked me to pick her up at the doctor's office and bring her to the hospital for further tests. The tests showed that she had lung cancer. She was sixty-one years old and a non-smoker, so the diagnosis was confusing. We explored several possibilities of a cause but eventually let go of that. The main thing was to figure out how to deal with it.

Two days later she had her first appointment with the oncologist. Since my parents had been divorced for many years, and Leslie, my only sibling, lived out of town, I would be my mom's main assistant through the illness.

My mom and I sat together in the small exam room in the oncologist's office building. The doctor greeted my mom with a handshake and smile. "Good afternoon." His gray hair was slicked back and he didn't seem in too much of a rush.

I wondered how day after day he worked with terminally ill patients and still maintained a positive outlook on life.

"By the time lung cancer is detected, often it is very late in the illness," he said. He mentioned that there was a lot of promising new research, but at that time 75 percent of lung cancer cases were fatal.

I tapped my foot rapidly and could feel my heart beating.

My mom stared silently at him, trying to take it all in. The information from the doctor took time to understand and integrate, if that was even possible.

"We will do everything we can to help you," he continued.

My mom relaxed back into her chair.

"But I also need to mention that now is the time to start preparing for the worst case scenario."

That caused my mom to sit straight up. She opened her eyes wide.

"Compared to similar cases, I would estimate you have six to twelve months left."

She stared straight ahead. A diagnosis like this was terrifying and devastating. It changes everything, all at once.

I rubbed my hand on my face.

She declined chemotherapy but decided to take radiation treatment since it could help to reduce the size of the tumor. This would relieve some pain and coughing.

I turned thirty-three the week after my mom's diagnosis, and I invited my girlfriend of two months to join my mom and me for a birthday dinner. I knew it would give my mom pleasure to see that I was going out with someone who was so pretty and nice. My mom had often told me that just because she and my father were divorced didn't mean marriage was bad. If the right person came along, I was definitely open to it.

After dinner I dropped my mom off and then drove my girlfriend home.

"Thanks for coming along tonight," I told her. "It meant a lot to my mom."

"It was fun," she said. "Your mom is great."

"Last week she was diagnosed with terminal lung cancer," I said.

There was long pause.

"Sorry to hear," she said.

We drove in silence the rest of the way.

We pulled up to her apartment.

She quickly said, "Goodbye," then left the car without looking back. No hug or goodnight kiss.

The next day I called and left a message but never got a call back.

The next week I tried again.

She picked up the phone. "I'm sorry, I can't handle your mom's illness right now."

"You don't have to do anything," I said.

"I just can't deal with it right now," she said. "I'm sorry."

My mom spent much of her time in the first two weeks getting organized. The prognosis she received from the oncologist was like a death sentence but also a blessing in its own way. It allowed her to take care of unfinished business and say goodbye to everyone. Six months was not a long time. An urgency settled in for both of us.

I tried to learn every detail of her life that I could, so when her capacity to manage her life diminished, I would be able to help. Becoming an expert at managing the ins and outs of her health insurance was essential. Her accountant told us that even for smaller estates like hers, it was financially beneficial to set up a trust. He recommended an attorney downtown who could help her with that.

When the trust was ready, we drove downtown to sign all the forms. In the car, my mom said, "I am making you the executor."

"OK, I am fine with that," I said.

"You'll also be co-owner and co-signer of my checking and safe deposit box," she said.

"I thought you would never ask."

She was all business. "You are good with details and follow-through, and you live in town."

We parked in a large ramp connected to the tall building

where the attorney's office was located. After a short wait, the attorney came out to get us.

"Nice to meet you in person," he said. My mom and he had talked on the phone, and she had mailed him the necessary information.

"This is my son," she said. We shook hands.

"Please follow me," he said.

The forms we had to sign were neatly laid out on a large table in the attorney's office.

After we were all seated, he stood up and pointed to each stack of papers as he moved around the table. "This is the will, the trust, the power of attorney, the living will, the healthcare power of attorney, and the letter of intent."

We took a few minutes to walk around the table and look them over.

"You will sign at the red arrows," he said to my mom. "And your son will sign at the yellow arrows."

On the way back to her apartment, the bright, summer sun lifted our spirits. We stopped at Pepito's, her favorite Mexican restaurant. She spoke between bites of the large chicken burrito. "Many siblings have broken apart when trying to divvy up the stuff that belonged to their parents," she said.

I took a bite of my cheese enchilada. "Aren't you jumping the gun a little? I mean, you're not gone yet."

"That's what's on my mind," she said. She took another bite and cherished every morsel.

"OK," I replied. Even before this diagnosis, occasionally she would give me instructions on how to proceed if anything happened to her. Several times over the years she showed me where she kept the ring she got from her father and the handwritten document that said she wanted to be cremated.

"This tastes amazing," she said.

We ate in silence for a few minutes.

"Not to worry," I said. "It will be easy for us. I have an empty condominium that can fit all your furniture, and Leslie doesn't need it. She wants the china and silverware, and I have no interest in it." Even though I knew the prognosis, I still couldn't believe it. My mom looked fine.

She laughed. "Maybe I'm not the only one who is jumping the gun."

One afternoon in late June, my mom was resting in bed when I stopped over for a visit. "I'm concerned you will have a tough time after I'm gone," she told me.

"I'll be fine." I had a nice condominium a half mile from Lake Harriet. And my job as a district-wide mentor teacher was the best one I ever had.

"You broke up with your girlfriend," she said.

The reminder caused a flash of sadness. "Maybe it was for the best," I said. The response I got when I told her about my mom's illness gave me a clue that she was probably not someone I could count on.

My mom slowly got out of bed, walked to the living room, and took a seat on the couch.

I went to the kitchen and poured each of us a glass of orange juice.

"I thought I would be OK too after each of my parents passed away." She closed her eyes as if she needed to take a nap.

"Do you want to be left alone?" I asked her.

"No, there is something else I need to tell you." She took a sip of the orange juice. "Even if you don't understand it now, please remember this. I really mean it with all my heart." She had tears in her eyes.

I could feel the tears well up in me too. "OK."

"No matter what happens, please remember that I love you and forgive you for everything."

By early July, the contrast in her health from only a month before was shocking. Besides losing some weight off her already thin frame, she also lost her ability to do her favorite activity. Walking fast around Lake Harriet had always given her so much pleasure. Only a few months before, I could not keep up with her walking pace. Now, the pain in her feet and the rest of her body would not allow her to continue. Her breathing became labored when walking the few yards from the parking lot to the path. Even getting out of bed in the morning was difficult. The heaviness of the illness slowed her down and sapped her energy.

During July, word of the illness spread from her close friends to her wider circle of acquaintances. In addition to the get-well cards that arrived each day, a parade of visitors stopped by her sunny suburban apartment. All the attention both uplifted and exhausted her. She put on her best face as they filled her in on the recent gossip and discussed current events. Inflation and interest rates were high. President George H. W. Bush was planning the Gulf War. Mikhail Gorbachev, leader of the Soviet Union, visited Minneapolis earlier in the summer and ate lunch at the same Pepito's where we liked to eat.

At the end of July, after an appointment with her oncologist, we drove by Pepito's. I pulled into the parking lot. "Do you want the chicken burrito again?"

"I can't eat anything right now."

"But remember what you said before. There is no such thing as a diet anymore. You can eat whatever you want."

"I'll have to pass for today," she said sadly.

☀

By the beginning of August, our roles started to shift. I was becoming more of the caretaker and parent. She lost interest in paying her bills and shopping for groceries. A lot of times I felt limited on what I could do to help. The illness progressed faster than we could have imagined, and there was nothing I could do to stop that. The violent coughing fits rattled and shook her frail body to the core. She moved slower, talked less, and wore the nasal oxygen cannula almost all the time.

After dropping off some groceries at her place at the end of the first week in August, we visited in the living room. She never talked about her feelings on death, but this time she opened up a little.

"It's hard for me to sleep much anymore," she said.

"Why, what's going on?" I asked.

"I feel like I'm always on guard."

"What do you mean?" I asked.

"I'm afraid if I go to sleep, I won't wake up," she said. "I don't want to fall asleep."

I said the only thing that came in my mind. "Sorry you have to go through all of this."

My emotions were buried as I tried to get through each day. Neither of us had any idea what was around the next corner. I did what needed to be done as it came my way. Each day was a different puzzle, and all we could do was try to figure it out, one piece at a time. The whole process was wearing me down.

Following the diagnosis, my sister, Leslie, came from Chicago every weekend she could. On my mom's sixty-second birthday, August 11, Leslie and I took her out to Lake Harriet on a picture-perfect day. The high was a sunny seventy-two degrees, and there was a light breeze. She had her nasal cannula on, and I carried the portable oxygen machine. As we walked slowly from the car to the lake, she explained exactly what we were to do after she passed. "I don't want a funeral. One of these plaques on the kiosk is enough. And you already know I want to be cremated. I prefer my ashes to go in the lake here."

We tried to go for a walk, but she could only go a few yards before getting too tired to continue. Instead, we sat on a bench by the lake. Leslie brought her popcorn and ice cream, two of her favorite Lake Harriet treats, but she wasn't hungry. The three of us stared in silence at the lake as we sat on the bench.

After a couple of minutes, I stood up. My mom said, "Wait a minute. Please." I sat back down. "There's something I need to tell you. Both of you are the best thing to ever happen to me. Thank you for being great kids." I could see a tear in her eye and felt one in mine. She coughed and needed to catch her breath. She smiled. "I'll never understand how two country club brats grew up to be social workers."

She leaned on my sister as we walked back to the car.

The trip to Lake Harriet on her birthday signaled the beginning of the end. Doing simple things like making meals and bathing became more difficult and time consuming. The visits from her friends ended. They still wanted to visit, but my mom did not want any visitors after that point. She had been an engaging, glamorous person, and she wanted her friends to remember her in that way. Now she was transitioning out of this world.

Two days after her birthday, whatever control over the situation we thought we had, was gone. She found blood in her stool and couldn't get an appointment to see her oncologist, so we went to the emergency room. They didn't know her history and were cautious on how to proceed. When she was finally transferred from the emergency room to a hospital bed, the test the doctor did was the most invasive one yet. For preparation she had to fast for several hours and take laxatives. The nurse also gave her an enema.

They performed the endoscopy as I sat in the waiting room across the hall. For the first time in my life, I could hear her yelling and screaming as if she were being tortured.

After it was all over, I joined her in the room. "What was going on in here?" I asked.

"I could tell I was making a lot of noise, but I couldn't help it," she said. "Whatever pills they gave me before the procedure made me feel like I lost my mind."

"It sounded like you were having a rough time," I said.

She could still muster up a smile. "So I gave a little show for all the people out there."

"Kind of, but I think they are used to that stuff in a hospital."

The nurse came in the room.

"What was the name of the sedative that the doctor gave my mom?" I asked.

The nurse told us the name.

My mom said to me, "Remember the name and never let them give it to me again."

They couldn't find the source of the bleeding. An invasive procedure like that was enough to drain her of the little remaining energy she had left. In her weakened state from the cancer, she did not have the strength to recover.

After three days she was allowed to leave the hospital, but before going, she got back the results of a full body CAT scan. The oncologist brought in a printout of the results and showed it to us. He didn't need to say anything. Both of us could see the dark spots indicating the cancer had spread from the lungs to several areas around her body.

We knew right away that it was over. For the first time in the process, both of us felt that all hope was gone. Losing hope of improvement is a terrible feeling at any time or place in life. This was the first time I experienced it in such a complete and final way. There was nothing a doctor could do for her anymore except try to keep her comfortable.

A hospital bed, grab bars, shower seat, and other needed equipment were delivered to her apartment. The soreness in her back and hips was agonizing whenever she tried to move, and she had to start taking pain pills to get through the day. She would have to learn to live with whatever was going wrong at the time. In addition to a nursing assistant sleeping at her apartment, regular day visits from nursing assistants and other caregivers were set up. This new arrangement only lasted for a week. At that point it was no longer feasible to stay at home. She moved to the hospice floor in the hospital.

Two days later, Leslie came from Chicago. She stayed with our mom for five straight nights in the hospital. By the sixth day, she was totally exhausted and desperately needed some rest. She had to go back to Chicago to tend to some pressing issues. Her plan was to return in three days.

By that point in time, our mom couldn't talk. The tears welled up in both their eyes as my sister gave her a big hug. She told our mom, "Hang in there. I love you so much." Then Leslie slowly turned toward the door like she didn't want to leave. She took one last glance before exiting the room.

After I dropped Leslie at the airport for her 7:00 p.m. flight, I decided to make one last stop at the hospital. The hospice nurse met me in the hall outside my mom's room.

She said, "I am so glad you came back. My best guess is that your mom only has twelve hours to live."

I glanced in the room but didn't notice any changes from an hour before. Apparently, after you have seen so many people die, you learn to predict such things.

"You need to stay the night," the nurse said.

I put my head down and rubbed my forehead. "I can't, I mean,

I don't think I can do it." I had a fear of sleeping in the hospital. The thought of being alone with her in the dying process was not comforting to me, to say the least. It challenged me like nothing else had ever challenged me before.

"You need to stay," the nurse repeated.

I took a jagged breath, swallowed hard, and walked into the room.

Her breathing was very loud and labored. She was on her back, and propped up on some pillows. I sat in the chair next to her and held her hand. She wasn't able to grab my hand, but now and then there was a very slight return pressure like she was checking to make sure I was still there. Her hand was cooler than mine, and it seemed to be getting colder with the passing of each hour. Over the next two hours, her breathing quieted down as it got shallower and shallower. There was no movement in her body. The breathing became a muffled gurgle in her throat. I leaned back in the chair.

After about three hours, I dozed off into a light sleep, but soon something in the energy of the room shifted, and it jerked me awake. I glanced at the clock and saw it was 2:20 a.m. Her hand was markedly colder, and I let my hand slip out of hers. There was absolutely no resistance. Her breathing was silent. I got up from the chair next to her bed, took a close look at her, and placed my hand on her eyes to close them. There was nothing more for me to do in the room. I grabbed her only personal items from the shelf. With her gray hooded sweatshirt in one hand and her purse in the other, I left the room. I told the nurses. From the phone in the hospital waiting room, I called my sister, the funeral home, her sister, and her best friend.

The parking ramp was almost empty so it was easy to find my car. The fifteen-minute drive to my condominium went fast, since the roads were not crowded at that time of the night. In the isolation of the car, I glanced at the front seat where I had set the purse and sweatshirt. The sobbing began, and I continued crying the rest of the drive home. Her death triggered something deep inside of me. All the emotions I held in over the summer flowed out in the tears.

Driving at that time of night was easy, but the thoughts in my mind were not. The events from the last three months replayed like a movie in my brain. I could not figure out how to deal with the extreme feelings of sadness. In some ways, the aftermath of the summer was more challenging than living through it the first time. Reality firmly set in. My mom was dead.

After a restless couple hours of sleep, I woke up at 6:00 a.m. The thought hit me that from the moment of conception, she and I had been on the planet at the same time. Now I was alone. In fifty years, when I was eighty, would I still remember her and miss her? Finding a way to integrate her death in my life seemed impossible. The sobbing I started in the car a few hours before continued on and off with no end in sight. The littlest thought or memory once again ignited the tears.

☀

After a few days, I needed to get back to work. Immersing myself in my job forced me to take my mind off the grieving, at least for a few hours a day. I taught middle school math for the first two hours of the day, and I was released from the classroom for the rest of the day to mentor new teachers around the district.

Away from work, I kept very busy taking care of all the needed organizational activities that we had so thoroughly planned before she died. Keeping a person's life going when they are incapacitated by a severe illness is very complicated, and it is just as complex to unravel it after they pass.

When I did have some quiet time away from work, I spent it re-living the memories from that summer and other times in her life. What my mom said to me about love and forgiveness became the main source of comfort for me, especially when I was feeling guilty.

Hindsight always makes it easier to see more clearly. If we had known from the start it would be a three-month illness, it might have impacted how all of us proceeded through the process. But death doesn't work that way. There is no such thing as a do-over, and it is very easy to fall into feeling guilty. One of the things I had second thoughts about was that I never moved in with her after the diagnosis. After she passed away, the thought gnawed at me that I may have been of much more comfort and help to her if I had done so.

Perhaps I was selfish for not moving in, but the thought of being immersed in the situation twenty-four hours a day was more than I could have handled. I didn't think I had the capacity to do it. Maybe this was true—maybe it wasn't. As the hospice nurse showed me on the night my mom died, sometimes your capacity is bigger than you think it is. What a great thing the nurse did by convincing me to stay with my mom on that last night. I remembered her first name, and two weeks after my mom died, I sent a card to the hospice floor:

Dear Maggie,

Thank you for going above and beyond when you encouraged me to stay the night with my mom, Barbara Hertz. Being with her when she passed was the most profound thing I ever experienced. I am sure it helped her too.

With sincere and deep gratitude,
Daniel Hertz

My mom's friends tried to help and did what they could for me. They invited me over for dinner and checked in often. They tried to fix me up on dates, but I wasn't close to being ready for that. I was still too emotionally fragile. How or if I would ever move beyond the grieving state of mind was a mystery to me. But to my surprise, it turned out I was helped through this process by an unexpected friend.

※

Two months after her passing, the guy upstairs in my condominium building asked, "Why don't you get a dog?" This was a thought that hadn't crossed my mind. Hearing the suggestion to get a dog from my condominium neighbor was especially surprising. He was a stickler for rules, and known to be very controlling. I couldn't believe he would allow the condo board to approve it. *Was it so obvious that even he could tell I was having a lot of trouble with the grieving process?*

Two days after he suggested it to me, a neighbor across the alley told me about a litter of golden retriever puppies that had recently been born one block away. I went to check it out. Six puppies played together in the middle of the kitchen floor. One sat alone in the corner. He had a small patch of white hair on his back left paw. I stared at him for a moment and felt the beginning of a smile. Even so, I was not certain enough at that point to make a decision to buy him.

Two weeks later, I went to visit the puppies again. There was only one left. I saw the white hairs on his back left paw. He greeted me as if he had been waiting for me. Since I still felt very drawn to him, I gave them the full price and went shopping for all the supplies.

The next night after work I picked him up and became a fully devoted parent. Friends commented that I treated the dog like my child. He and I became very close, very fast. He learned the tricks like "sit" and "stay" so quickly that he seemed like a "natural." That is where the name came from. I named him Roy after the lead character from the book and movie entitled *The Natural*.

Roy didn't like the normal roughhousing with other dogs. Often I brought him to the dog park, and when the roughhousing started, he would sit by me until it was over. He didn't like the game of fetch, even though he was a golden retriever. After one or two tries, he would look at me as if to say, *this is silly, do we have to continue?* All his quirky behavior reinforced the feeling that something was different about this dog.

The bond between Roy and me became stronger over time. He came with me everywhere it was possible to bring him. After moving back to Minneapolis from Texas, I rented a small studio apartment and saved up enough money for a down payment on three acres of densely wooded land in the St. Croix River Valley. Whenever I went to my cabin in the woods, Roy would accompany me.

Roy even came with me to my middle school math classroom. It was an incredible help to the atmosphere in the class to have a dog in the room. He would roam up and down the rows, and it made it feel like a friendlier, homier atmosphere. When a kid was having a tough day, they would sit with him in the corner until they felt better.

He not only helped the students in my classes, he guided me through the grieving and healing process. The devotion and care I gave Roy allowed me to occasionally move outside of my intense inner focus on sadness and despair.

That is when I started to think deeper about the connection between my mom and Roy. If it was possible, through Roy, my mom continued to teach and help me.

CHAPTER FIVE

The Meditation Center

COURAGE — Practice the Lion's pose to have the courage to say what needs to be said. (Sit in the kneeling posture with the top of the feet on the floor and the buttocks resting on the heels. Place the palms of the hands just above the knees. Lift the body slightly off the heels and lean forward at the same time that you straighten the arms, open the mouth as wide as possible and thrust the tongue down and out. Make a sound from deep in the throat as the tongue is out.)

I n March of 1992, my morning work alarm went off. When I tried to sit up in bed, I writhed from a sharp pain in my lower back. As I reached to the right to turn off my alarm, my neck got stuck, like a lid on a jar that wouldn't open. I stood up, and the ache in my knees caused me to wobble. On my first step, the bottoms of my feet were so tender that it was difficult to walk. I was only thirty-four but felt like I was eighty years old. After I slowly made my way to the kitchen, I reached up to grab a bowl from the shelf, and I recoiled from the stabbing sensation in my shoulder. A year and a half had passed since my mom died. The physical problems that started after her death continued to worsen. I knew I needed to do something. It took two weeks to get an appointment for a physical.

In the small exam room, I wore a hospital gown and sat across from the doctor. "Well, your prostate is normal," he said. "No sign of hernia, blood pressure is good, and your weight is fine." He wrote something in my file. "You'll get your blood test results in a couple of days. Anything else I can do for you today?"

"When I try to get out of bed in the morning, my lower back hurts so much that it is difficult to even sit up. My neck is so . . . "

He looked at his watch. "Excuse me, I need to check on something." He left the room.

Five minutes later he returned. "You were saying?"

"My back is killing me, my neck is so stiff that I can hardly turn it, it is difficult to walk because my knees . . . "

He again said, "Excuse me for a minute." He left the room. I got cold in the flimsy gown, and there was no magazine in sight. *This is taking forever.*

Another five minutes passed, and when he returned, I was silent. I gave up trying to explain.

He wrapped things up by saying, "I'll send you a letter with your blood test results." He stood up, gathered some papers, and took the two steps to the door. He reached for the door handle and turned around. "Oh, and take a couple of Advil whenever you are sore." He smiled, nodded in my direction, and left the room.

The experience with the doctor was so aggravating that it turned me off to conventional medicine. Even I knew that Advil was not the solution, only a temporary band-aid. I started to wonder if I would ever find anything that could help me. As my mom learned to accept all the issues in her body, I began to think I would need to accept all my problems and make any needed lifestyle adjustments. At a relatively young age, I was not yet ready to accept that outcome.

The only strategy I could think of was to experiment with alternative treatments. When I did a search in the public library for books on alternative medicine, nothing helpful came up. I had to become my own health care manager. Mostly I learned from trying a lot of things. I started with deep tissue massage because it was offered at the YWCA where I had a membership. One thing led to another. Now and then a friend would recommend a practitioner they liked. Chiropractic adjustments were next. That led to acupuncture, herbs, homeopathy, and osteopathy. Each practitioner had a different recommendation. One said to eat meat, another said vegetarian was best, and others suggested various vitamin or juice supplements. The mind-body relationship was a new concept to me. Figuring out any cause and effect was complicated.

Shortly after the physical, I applied to graduate school. If accepted, my plan was to apply for a sabbatical leave for the following school year. My two-year term as a mentor teacher had ended the year before, and I was back to full-time teaching. After three years of teaching elementary school in Texas and eight years of middle school math in Minneapolis, burnout was encroaching. Teaching was very rigid. You had the same class at the same time every day. I wanted very much to continue as an educator, but I longed for a job where I could use the bathroom whenever I needed to go, rather than waiting for my prep hour. Showing students how to add and subtract fractions was, without a doubt, rewarding and super helpful in its own way. But often the social/emotional issues interfered with their learning. I wanted to focus my time on teaching positive goal setting and responsible decision making. In my heart, I knew I could be a great school counselor and was very motivated to pursue it.

In August of 1992, five months after that painful morning, my sabbatical leave started. I became a full-time graduate student in school counseling. Since I was trying to fit all the required master's degree classes and internship into one year, my graduate school schedule was packed. When I wasn't in class, I was busy reading textbooks and articles and preparing all the assignments. At the same time I was in graduate school, I continued the weekly body treatments that I had started several months before.

Becoming a counselor was a very difficult transition for me. Some other graduate students in the program had been through intensive counseling themselves. All of it was brand new to me. Sharing my feelings and reflecting on what others were feeling did not come naturally to me.

The group counseling course was especially challenging. Everyone in the class took a turn leading a practice session and choosing the topic for the session while the rest of us were participants. The professor watched and graded us through a two-way mirror.

At the end of the second week of the semester, the group counseling session topic was Death of a Loved One. The student leader began to her left and then continued around the circle. "What is your experience with the death of a loved one?" she asked everyone.

My turn came to answer. "I have some experience with that, but I am not comfortable sharing at this time." I didn't trust the student leader to handle my information, and the group environment did not feel safe enough. Group members needed to feel that what they were saying would be heard without judgment. Reaching this comfort level took time and could not be forced.

As the semester progressed, I became more comfortable with the people and the process. I was able to contribute more on easier topics like Job Burnout.

After the last class of the first semester, my group counseling professor pulled me aside and said she needed to speak to me.

We were seated in her small office. She was behind her desk, and I sat in a plastic-bottomed chair on the other side of the desk. I leaned against the back of the chair to support my tender lower back.

"How do you think the semester went?" she asked.

She had never asked me to go into her office before, so I

was a little surprised with the sudden interest. I moved my backpack from my lap to the floor and crossed my legs.

"It has been very busy," I replied. I looked forward to some much needed rest over the upcoming winter break.

"I've decided to give you an Incomplete for the class," the professor said.

My head jutted forward, my mouth opened, and I raised my eyebrows. There was a shooting pain in my lower back and my jaw tightened.

She twirled a pen quickly in her right hand. "I don't feel you disclosed enough about yourself in the class group counseling sessions."

I was stunned into silence. A grade of Incomplete would not allow me to start the internship at Washburn High School that I had set up for spring semester. From my experience as a teacher, I knew that most counselors in Minneapolis did not run group counseling sessions, so it was difficult to understand why this was a prerequisite.

She hastily straightened some papers on her desk.

"But what can I do to complete what you need from me?" I asked. "It's the last day of class."

"I don't know," she responded. "You'll have to figure that out. Is there anything else I can do for you today?" She stood up.

I grabbed my backpack and shuffled out the door.

There was a pain in my heart as I walked down the hall. The stabbing sensation returned to my lower back, and the ache in my neck was screaming out. All the benefits of the last eight months of body work washed away.

The only thing I could think of was to track down my graduate school advisor. Fortunately, I caught him in his office before he left for his winter break. He was one of four professors in the department.

I explained to him what had happened a few minutes before with the other professor. He shook his head slowly, frowned, rolled his eyes, sighed, and checked his watch. "I'll talk to her and the other two professors before they leave for break. Give me a call later this afternoon."

Later that day I called my advisor from the phone at the little desk in my condominium. "The other two professors and I want to support you," he said. "The group counseling professor has agreed to let the three of us make the decision on how to proceed."

By that time I had already come up with an idea that I presented to him. "What if I do a group counseling session with any students who are left in the campus dorm over winter break? I'll videotape it and write it up to show all of you."

"Sounds like a really good idea. Go ahead and plan on it and I'll let the others know."

My posting in the dormitory got enough responses to hold the group session. The twelve participants were international students who had no choice but to stay in the dorm during break. The topic I picked for the hour-long group session was Dealing with Loneliness.

Everyone sat in a circle, and I started the video recorder. I went over the group rules and how important it was to keep everything confidential. "Let's go around the room. Please share something that has helped you deal with loneliness."

The first person said, "I keep as busy as I can with my studies, but over break I have more time."

"Over break you are more likely to feel lonely," I said. This was a common counseling technique called reflection of feelings.

"That's correct," he said.

In early January I submitted the tape to the professors to pass around to each other. I never heard back from the group counseling professor, but the other three all agreed it was fine and that they would allow me to start the internship.

The first day of my internship at Washburn was on January 20, 1993, the day of Bill Clinton's inauguration. On the tour around the school, some of the teachers had a television tuned into the event. As we walked, my supervising counselor explained to me that a large part of my time in the internship would be to assist in the running of the peer mediation/peaceful conflict resolution program.

In the beginning of March, the "I" grade on my transcript still hadn't been changed. After getting home from a day at the internship, I called the group counseling professor. "Can you change my grade now? The other professors thought my tape was OK." I moved my head slowly from side to side to try and relieve the tightness in my neck.

"I saw the tape, and I didn't think it was good enough," she said.

I slouched in the chair. "But I thought you said if they approved it, it would be OK with you."

"Well, I don't think it is good enough. I need to go. There is another student in my office I need to talk to."

The sting of helplessness in the face of authority hung in the air. It jabbed at my lower back and squeezed my temples. The grade of "I" weighed heavily on my mind and already fragile body. Getting through the graduate program was incredibly important to me. I had devoted a lot of time and money in taking a year off of work and going back to school, and hated the thought of it going down the drain.

Even though my supervising counselor at Washburn did not run any group counseling sessions, when I told him about the situation the next day, he was very supportive. I immediately started to organize some sessions for students who had failed a class in the previous quarter. The topic was Academic Success Strategies.

I videotaped each of the three group counseling sessions, made a transcript of what was said, and by each line on the transcript I named the counseling theory I used. Again I submitted the tape and transcript to all four professors. Three of the professors said it looked good, but once more I never heard back from the group counseling professor.

In late April I checked my transcript and the grade was still not changed. I called the professor again. "Do you have a minute to talk?"

"Yes, I suppose I have time," she said.

"The grade of Incomplete is still on my transcript. I can't graduate without it."

"I know that," she responded.

"You wanted us to learn how to give feedback in the group counseling process, right?" I asked.

"Yes," she said quickly.

"Well, I have some feedback for you," I said.

That was met with silence. I waited a few moments, and when she didn't respond, I continued.

"You gave me an Incomplete on the last day of class without any warning before that. That is not fair. If you had told me earlier that my skills weren't good enough, maybe I would have had time to improve."

"OK, I'll put your grade on," she said angrily. "Goodbye." She hung up.

When I checked with the records office on campus at the end of the week, a grade of "C" was on my transcript. The "C" was like a fail in graduate school, but since it was my only "C" for the year, it was good enough to get my master's degree. Relief washed over me. I shook the hand of the surprised records clerk and told her she made my day.

After I drove home and was inside my condominium with the door closed, I hollered a piercing, joyful, "Whewhooooooo!" Roy joined me with a loud bark, a smile, and a rapid swishing of his tail. Now I was eligible to apply for any school counselor opening in the district and the M.S. degree meant a substantial pay increase.

A few days later, in early May of 1993, there was an article in the Minneapolis *StarTribune* about yoga. They interviewed a man who had recovered from severe back injuries through the practice of yoga.

On that same day, I had a previously scheduled appointment with my osteopath. Osteopaths manipulate muscles like chiropractors manipulate bones.

"Did you see that article in the paper today about yoga?" I asked.

He replied, "I haven't seen it yet."

"Do you think yoga could help me?"

"You are still recovering from all the injuries," he said.

The aches and pains that started three years before with the passing of my mom were still with me. I still couldn't raise my arm over the height of my shoulder. Walking Roy was difficult because of my aching knees and the tenderness in my feet.

"If you want to try yoga," he continued, "I would try a gentle style like they teach at the Meditation Center."

※

Going to a place like the Meditation Center was not something that had ever crossed my mind. In fact, I had never even heard of it.

A few months before, I had overheard a woman in the whirlpool at the YWCA talking to a mutual friend. "I started studying meditation, and I think it is helping," she said.

I laughed and said, "You mean like this, 'OOOOOMMMMMMMMMMM.'"

She gave me a look and said, "Not like that. They teach you to focus on your breath."

"OK," I replied. "How does that help?"

"Never mind," she said.

When I thought of yoga or meditation, I imagined pictures of agile people in difficult positions. I couldn't imagine something like that would ever be something I would try.

Even so, based on the recommendation from the osteopath, I decided to call the Meditation Center to get some more information on what they offered.

"What is the best class to start with?" I asked.

"The combined yoga and meditation is nice if this is your first class," the receptionist said. "A new session starts next Wednesday."

I gave her my name and address, and she promised to mail a brochure right away.

A couple of days later the brochure arrived. Usually the first thing I did after work was make dinner, but instead I laid on the bed, turned on the reading lamp, and looked over the brochure. Near the top it said the Meditation Center had been located in the same place in northeast Minneapolis since it was established in 1970. The yoga postures were mainly seen as a preparation of the body for the sitting meditation practice, rather than as an exercise in itself. Clearly highlighted was that the Himalayan Tradition is an ancient, unbroken lineage of the Raja Yoga system. It is a science and a philosophy that does not require adherence to a particular religion, dogma, or belief system. That was a relief. I wasn't looking for a new religion. Even though I was not active in a synagogue, I strongly identified as being Jewish.

The following week I went to the first class. The Meditation Center was in an old, mansion style, brick building that many years before had housed the nuns associated with the church across the street. There was a small sign in the window of the foyer door: *The custom of removing our shoes is symbolic of leaving dirt and discord behind as we turn toward the experience of peace and harmony.* I entered the large foyer. To my right there was a small office with a couple of desks and some office equipment. To the left there was a small bookstore and also a coat and shoe rack. The woman in the office greeted me. "Welcome to the center."

"Thanks. Is there still room in the class for tonight?"

"Definitely," she replied.

I filled out all the required forms and waited in the classroom.

After a few minutes, several other students arrived. We sat on chairs that were arranged in a semi-circle on the carpeted floor. The lights were dimmed a little, and a refillable oil candle wick was lit in the corner. The room still had a lot of the original wood window frames, baseboards, and molding. In the back corner, there were several large, neat piles of small pillows and blankets stacked against the wall.

The instructor greeted us as he entered the room. He was a young man, probably in his early twenties. "Welcome, everybody." He smiled as he looked around. "I returned last week from six months in India, so I am still having some culture shock." He sat cross-legged on some pillows in the front of the room and closed his eyes. The six women and two guys in the class were quietly staring at him for a couple of minutes. *Does he just sit there for the whole class?*

When he finally spoke again, the sound of his voice startled me. I leaned back in my chair and crossed my arms.

"But before we begin, I would like to hear a little bit about all of you and why you came today."

The students ranged in age from about thirty to sixty years old. One was a physical therapist, another an architect. There was also an artist, psychologist, and office manager. They came because they heard yoga was good for stress and that it was good exercise.

I uncrossed my arms when it was my turn to speak. "I need something to help me with the stress of work, and my body is sore all over."

"Alright," the instructor said. "Good to meet all of you. Could everybody please stand up, next to the chair?"

We started with some stretches. The other students seemed to be doing OK, but I almost left after the first few minutes. The pain and tightness in my lower back kicked in when I barely started a simple forward bend. I was sad that once again I would have to keep searching for something that could help.

"Sir," the instructor said. "I can see you are having a hard time."

"That's correct," I said. "Every time I try to bend over, it's killing me."

"Not to worry," he responded. "Here's what we can do. If everybody could please move into the mountain or *tadasana* posture." He demonstrated standing fully upright, but not stiff. "It is the most difficult posture to master."

"Why are we starting out with the hardest posture?" I asked.

The instructor replied, "It is the hardest to master. Not the hardest to do. Please give it a try."

I stood up straight with my feet shoulder-width apart, and let my arms dangle at the side, exactly like the instructor was doing. *This is the hardest to master? Even I can do it.*

"Now, if everyone can have a seat in the chair next to where you are standing, we will move on to the joints and glands exercise series. These are simple exercises that hopefully everyone can do."

"You mean even if someone has a lot of pain?" I interrupted.

"They should be OK for you. The exercises are simple and very gentle. They can help with circulation and flexibility in various areas of your body such as the neck, shoulder, back, and knees."

Everyone sat in a chair, and the instructor continued. "OK,

good, please sit up straight with your feet flat on the floor." He glanced around the room. "Looks good. On the next inhalation, raise your shoulders as high as they can go. On the next exhalation, let them drop quickly, but keep your exhalation slow." He watched all of us. "This is called the shoulder shrug." We repeated it several times and then moved on to the next exercise. The instructor reminded us often to deepen and slow our breath. When my back hurt from sitting up, I leaned against the back of the chair. The series of about thirty exercises took about an hour and a half to finish.

It surprised me that these exercises were something I could actually do. I didn't know any exercises like this existed. They ignited something inside of me and I couldn't wait to start practicing them at home. To help us remember them, at the end of class, the instructor gave us a sheet to take home with stick figures doing the exercises. Since I had started my summer break two days earlier after finishing the year of full-time graduate school, I had time to practice.

Beginning the next day, I practiced those joints and glands exercises for an hour in the morning and an hour at night. I was thrilled to finally find something I could do to help myself.

The next week I returned to class. The instructor welcomed us. "Good to see everyone again. The key to doing the joints and glands exercises is coordinating the movements with the breathing." This type of breath awareness is how yoga is different from other types of exercise. "From your seated position, let your arms hang at the side. Inhale when you tense your fist and exhale when you release it." He demonstrated, and then everyone tried it. "This has a much different result than simply opening and closing your hand."

When I tried to release the tension in my fist at the same time as the long exhalation, my shoulders dropped, my forehead smoothed out, my jaw released, and my arm went limp.

After I finished the six-week summer yoga class, I interviewed for and got a school counselor job at Susan B.

Anthony Middle School. When I started the job in August, there was a steep learning curve. The constant onslaught of parent phone calls and schedule changes was challenging, but I was happy with the change. I still felt like a teacher, but in a little different way.

Before and after work I continued to practice yoga and meditation at home and attended every class I could at the center. Even though I was making some progress with the joints and glands, I was still having a tough time with the meditation and guided relaxations. It took every ounce of determination I had to sit or lay still for even a few minutes during these activities. And sitting up straight in the chair for more than a couple of minutes, without back support, continued to be very painful.

In October, a month after the start of my new counseling job, the workload started to slow down a little bit. One day a quiet, small, red-headed boy with freckles and thick glasses stopped by my office. He handed me his pass and sat down across from me.

"What can I help you with today?" I asked him.

"Nothing," he said.

I rubbed my chin with my hand and looked expectantly at him with raised eyebrows.

"I didn't come to see you," he said.

Maybe he just needs a time-out. I turned to look at my computer.

"I came to see Roy," he said.

Roy's kennel was under the table in my office.

"You know how to open it?" I asked.

He nodded.

"Go ahead," I said.

His face lit up with a smile. He got down on the floor and gave Roy a big hug.

If Roy could have learned how to make class schedules, I'm pretty sure he would have taken over my whole job.

☀

In November, six months after first coming to the Meditation Center and doing the joints and glands routine for two hours a day, I could do a pain-free forward bend as soon as I got out of bed in the morning. While standing up and bending forward at the waist, my palms could touch flat on the floor for the first time in my life. Being able to do the forward bend without pain showed me that improvement was possible, and I was very encouraged to keep practicing.

There was no need for me to move from the chair to the floor for meditation practice, but after seven months of practice, I wanted to give it a try. I sat down on a mat with a few support pillows and set the kitchen timer for five minutes. My mind jumped around like crazy, my knees and ankles ached, and I wasn't able to sit up straight. When the timer went off and I opened my eyes, Roy was sitting in front of me. He was a big dog, and our eyes were at about the same level.

After that, every time I sat down to practice, he would join me. Seeing him as I opened my eyes reminded me to lighten up and not take the numerous thoughts floating through my mind so seriously.

※

Ten months after my first visit to the center, in the early spring of 1994, Roy and I took a Saturday night visit to my cabin. I went to bed at 9:00 p.m. The only light in the upstairs room was from the waxing crescent moon shining in the window. The closed windows blocked out any noises from the forest. While lying in bed, my quiet breathing was the only sound I could hear. Sleep met me very quickly. The next time I came to awareness, it took me a moment to notice that my mind was awake, but my body was asleep. I could not move. But instead of panic, I felt calm and saw myself in a different way than ever before. I was only a breathing organism, nothing more and nothing less. Then the sound of a chain clunked against the wooden floor.

The noise was enough to jar my body awake. It was difficult to know, but perhaps I was only in that state for a few moments. Roy's collar made the sound as he shifted his position on the floor. Then I heard the familiar sound of his clicking nails as he walked toward the bed. He stood by the bed, and from the light of the moon I could see his tail wagging. His head rested on the blanket as he looked up at me. I glanced at the clock; it was midnight. As I lay my head back on the pillow, I was filled with a new kind of energy. My mind was buzzing as I tried to figure out what had happened. Never before had I experienced my body and mind in that way. Then this thought came crashing into my mind: Is this all there is?

For the first time in my life, it was like I woke up. I wondered what I had been doing with my life for the last thirty-six years. A clear pattern emerged. My whole life looked like a series of repetitive movements. Eat. Sleep. Talk. Move around. Work. Repeat the next day.

During a couple of hours of racing thoughts before falling asleep, I continued to wonder what had happened. It wasn't an out-of-body experience. Instead, I had stumbled on a different state of awareness and the whole experience was very strange.

The next morning as I packed up my pick-up truck, everything seemed to have returned to normal. Roy sat next to me on the bench seat and I drove the eighty miles back to Minneapolis.

One month later, in May of 1994, after eleven months of yoga practice, I finally reached a very slightly deeper relaxation state in a guided relaxation in one of the classes at the center. Over and over the instructor asked the class to relax various parts of the body. In a slow, calm voice, he said, "Relax your forehead . . . relax your jaw . . . relax your shoulders . . . relax your fingers, your forearms, elbows, biceps . . . " And on and on and on, over and over again for the whole body. After thirty minutes, I was able to let go of tension I didn't even realize I was holding. My face went slack, my shoulders flattened against the floor, and I noticed that my breathing moved to a slower rate. The same thing happened in my mind. I wasn't aware that my thoughts were in a constant march or what it felt like to pause them, but for a moment, they paused, and the vacuum in my mind filled with joy. This state of relaxation only lasted for a second before the next worry charged into my thoughts. The tension in my body also returned. But that moment of relaxation was enough time for a thought I had never had before to slip clearly into my mind: This is my destiny.

CHAPTER SIX

Goodbye to Dad

LETTING GO — Practice arm swings to let go of
what you no longer need. (One variation is to stand
in the mountain pose and swing one arm forward
and one back, as if you are moving the arms in an
exaggerated walk.)

In June 1994, a month after that guided relaxation, I sat
by my dad's hospital bed in San Diego. Every so often he
would wake up for a few minutes, and we had a chance
to visit a little.

He glanced at the TV. "Why are they showing a white Ford
Bronco going down the highway?" he asked.

"Oh, I think O. J. Simpson is riding in it with someone," I replied.

"But why is he being chased by all the police and helicopters?"

"I don't know," I told him.

"That's strange," he said.

I nodded in agreement.

About thirty minutes later, he again opened his eyes and
glanced at the TV. "Why are they still chasing him?" he asked.
"There must be twenty police cars."

"I know, it's crazy. They said they wanted to speak to him about the murder of his ex-wife and her friend."

Another hour passed. He again opened his eyes, glanced at the clock, then the TV. "Still?"

They switched to a news conference and O. J.'s friend Robert Kardashian was reading a letter from O.J.: "Don't feel sorry for me . . . " the letter started.

After two hours, O. J. was taken into custody. The incident was watched on television by ninety-five million people.

☀

The call from my Uncle Sam had come two days earlier. "You need to get out here as soon as possible," he said.

Uncle Sam lived near my dad in a suburb of San Diego, and I had asked him to let me know when my dad got to the point where he couldn't take care of himself. If possible, I preferred to go there when I really needed to and stay, rather than flying back and forth a lot. As I knew from my mom, the timeline of the death process was not entirely predictable.

I told my principal what happened and made plans to fly out to San Diego from Minneapolis the night I heard from my uncle. My neighbor who helped babysit Roy over the years said it would be OK to leave him with her while I was out of town. I tried to let my dad know I was coming, but he didn't answer the phone.

Six months before, my seventy-three-year-old dad was playing handball and golf every other day. The last time I saw him was over spring break, a couple of months earlier. At that time he still lived in his condominium, but all he had the energy for was an easy, short walk in the morning. When he would receive a blood transfusion for the leukemia, he would be much better. As time went on, he needed the transfusions more often, and he would get noticeably more tired between treatments.

From the airport I took a midnight shuttle to the assisted living apartment where he was now staying. I had to knock on his apartment door to get in. It took a lot of knocking and at least ten minutes for him to come to the door. When he did make it, it was a sight I was not prepared to see. He looked so old and sick and thin compared to only two months before. Slowly, he made his way back to the bedroom without saying anything.

The only place for me to sleep was on the couch, and no sheets were in sight. Before lying down, I sat on the edge of the couch. After one year of practicing meditation, I was in the habit of sitting when I woke up in the morning and before I went to bed. I tried to slow my breath and relax my forehead, jaw, and shoulders. Thoughts from the hectic day and the look of my dad relentlessly floated through my mind. The day before I received that call from my uncle, it started to sink in for me how sick my dad must have been. For the first time in my thirty-seven years, my birthday came and went and I didn't receive a card or call from him. As I tried to fall sleep, I wondered what I would be facing the next day.

In the morning I tried to visit and catch up with my dad, but he wasn't in the mood for talking. He was struggling to move about and do the basic things that most people take for granted. Getting dressed and washing were a challenge. I borrowed his car and did some errands for him. We tried going out for an early dinner, but he wasn't able to eat anything.

The second day after I arrived, I called his doctor's office to ask how to proceed. The doctor returned my call right away. He said he would call ahead and that we should go to the emergency room for an immediate blood transfusion. Before leaving for the hospital, I called the attorney who was helping my dad organize his assets into a trust. On the way to the hospital, we stopped at the attorney's office. She met us at the curb, and he signed a couple of needed documents. One was his living will health care directive and another gave me power of attorney.

After the transfusion, he was transferred to a regular hospital room. A hospital attendant wheeled him to the room, and I walked alongside them. When we got to the room, he was exhausted but had to urinate. He wasn't stable enough to walk on his own, so he leaned against me as we walked the few steps to the bathroom. I held him up, and helped him steady his hand while he went. After he got settled into his bed, the nurse came by and offered him some juice and cookies. He perked up a little after the snack, but still felt like taking a nap. That night we watched the O. J. scene on television.

On my third day, the doctor came to his room. "You can continue the transfusions if you continue with the remaining treatment option," he told my dad. "The next step would be to surgically remove your spleen." He looked at my dad for a moment before continuing. "You remember we discussed this option in my office a couple of months ago?"

My dad nodded.

"Well, the time has come to make a decision," the doctor said.

My dad hadn't told me about that option. I stared at the doctor, with my eyebrows raised, trying to take in what he said.

The doctor glanced at his watch. "Think about it, and I'll be back in a minute."

I followed the doctor into the hallway. "How can he handle an operation in his condition?"

"That is up to your dad," he said.

All I could picture in my mind was him dying on the operating table, and what a terrible way that would be to end his life.

The doctor returned to the room to talk to my dad while I waited in the hall. I knew if I went in the room I would push for him to decline the operation. The doctor was right. At this point it really was my dad's decision to make, not mine.

While the doctor was speaking to my dad, a nurse was outside his room. "Do you think my dad can handle an operation in his condition?" I asked her. "I am really concerned he wouldn't survive the procedure."

She nodded.

When the doctor came out several minutes later, he took me aside. "Your dad has decided to go ahead with the operation."

My neck ached from the tension. I moved my head slowly from side to side and tried to think of something to say. "Do you think my dad is in a proper state of mind to make a decision like that?"

He paused for a moment. "I am not sure, but it is your dad's life we are talking about."

"OK, but if he has the operation, what is the expected outcome?" I asked.

Before the doctor could answer me, out of the corner of my eye, I saw someone exit his room.

It was the nurse I talked to in the hallway a few minutes before. She came over to the doctor and me. "Mr. Hertz told me he doesn't want the operation," she said.

The doctor went back in the room with her as I again waited in the hall. When they came out, the doctor told me my dad repeated to them that he didn't want the operation. It was the doctor's job to do everything possible to keep someone alive for as long as possible. On the other hand, there comes a time in every terminal illness when a decision had to be made on when to stop treatments. The moment of giving in to the fight and accepting imminent death is a personal and heart-wrenching decision. If possible, leaving the world in a gentle, quick way once the illness gets to a certain point is the preferred way to go. As I learned with my mom's passing, the finality of death can cause all sorts of intense emotions. Feeling guilty is easy. There is no do-over. I hoped the decision my dad made that day was the right one.

☀

Once the decision was made to decline further treatment, he immediately was enrolled into the hospice program. Twenty minutes later, three hospice workers showed up in his hospital room. The social worker would make arrangements with the nursing home, someone else would help with the health insurance forms, and the chaplain asked me if I needed to talk about spiritual concerns. It was comforting for both my dad and me to have the immediate support of all those people. The plan was for him to transfer to a nursing home in the same complex as his assisted living apartment.

Before checking out of the hospital, I was able to track down the nurse who helped me. "Thank you so much for helping with that decision about my dad's spleen surgery. You have no idea what it means to me."

"I was happy to be of help," she said. "It really made the most sense for me. Sometimes patients in your father's generation have trouble saying 'no' to a doctor."

We shook hands.

"Good luck with everything," she said. She reminded me of the nurse who helped me so much by convincing me to stay at the hospital the last night with my mom.

I drove my dad to the nursing home and helped him settle into his new room. Then I picked up a few supplies that he needed from his apartment. That night in his apartment, I called my sister in Chicago. "Here we go again. Dad entered hospice today."

She responded softly. "OK, thanks for letting me know."

"The doctor wanted to remove his spleen as a last resort, but dad declined. Are you OK with that?"

She answered without hesitation. "Yes, that is where the medical system is broken. The end of life trauma and expenses are crazy."

Her agreement with the decision my dad made to decline the surgery reinforced for me that we had done the right thing.

"You are welcome to come and help," I said. "But I am totally OK being here on my own." A month before I had arrived, she had come to San Diego for a few days and helped my dad move from his condominium to the assisted living unit.

"That works for me," she said. "Thanks. I'll let you know if I change my mind."

Everyone reacts differently to the impending death of a loved one. There is no right or wrong way to proceed.

"OK, I'll keep in touch with any developments," I said.

The next day, four days after I arrived, he awoke after a nap and was a little groggy. He was not taking any medications and his mind was fine, but everything he went through in the last few days was a little disorienting. I was reading by his bed.

"What is going on?" he asked. "Why I am still in the nursing home?"

I reminded him that he was in hospice and would not have any more transfusions.

He nodded. "So that's the game."

It sunk in for both of us that there was nothing more that could be done to help him. The same feeling of hopelessness and resignation I had during my mom's illness settled in on me once again.

The fifth day he had an unexpected visitor. A woman who he knew from high school lived in the area and heard from a mutual friend that he was very sick. My dad was fading in and out of sleep, but whenever he opened his eyes, he gave a smile of recognition to what the woman was saying. She was looking through an old book of photos I found in his apartment and was reminiscing about the pictures.

Every night, after visiting with him during the day, I returned to his assisted living apartment. I sorted through all his clothing, boxes of old pictures, and other things he had accumulated over the years. The myriad decisions on what to keep and what to give away were grinding me down. Everything was spread out on the floor in a mess as I tried my best to get it organized. Sitting for meditation each night helped me sort through some of the various intense emotions I had as my dad deteriorated every day.

On the ninth day, I came in the morning, as usual, to see how he was doing. I was surprised to see he was dressed, shaven, and sitting on the side of the bed, eating his favorite breakfast of poached eggs. He looked great. "Let's go back to my apartment and get out of this place," he said.

How was this possible? He was knocking on death's door just yesterday. I paced the floor.

"I am sorry, I can't do that," I said. "The doctor said you need to stay in this place. They can help you with a lot of things here that I can't do at home."

"Please take me out of here," he pleaded.

Oh, my God. Now what do I do? I sat down in the chair by his bed and buried my face in my hands. More than anything I wanted to help him. But even if he was OK, I couldn't bring him back to the assisted living apartment. The place was turned upside down. I dug around in my pocket, found the card the hospice social worker had given me, and gave her a call from the phone in his room.

"Can you at least wait for the hospice people?" I asked. "They said they were on the way." He agreed to that and sat back down on the bed. Fortunately, the social worker and hospice nurse arrived within fifteen minutes. They must have dropped whatever else they were doing when they heard the panic in my voice.

The three of us sat down around him. "Mr. Hertz, what your son is saying is true. It is best for your care if you stay here. You need the help that is offered in the nursing home." That reassurance calmed him down and he stopped asking to leave.

The hospice people left after a few minutes, and I stayed with him.

When I came to visit the next morning, he again was in his bed. He looked pale, thin, and frail, and could not sit up in bed on his own. All he could do was lift his chin as he saw me walk in the room.

On the eleventh day, I asked my dad something that had been on my mind. "If you can, will you wait for me? I would like to be with you when the time is right."

He nodded.

Nothing more needed to be said. He knew exactly what I meant.

A phone call from the nursing home came at 7:30 the next morning. His vital statistics had changed significantly overnight. I prepared to go in and stay the whole day with him. When I arrived at 10:30 a.m., there was a nurse and two nursing assistants standing by his bed. They told me his blood pressure was zero and his pulse had almost stopped, but he was still alive.

"Could you please leave the room?" I asked. "I would like to be alone with him." After they left, I took his hand and told him I loved him. He started to talk and said "I love . . . " then he was gone. His last word was "love."

I made quick calls from his room to my sister, Uncle Sam, and a cousin to tell them the news. The nursing home took care of all the arrangements for shipping the body back to St. Paul for the funeral.

As I walked back to his apartment with tears in my eyes, these words came into my mind: Good night. Good luck. I love you. I hadn't thought of them for twenty-five years. These were the words my father and I said to each other each night when I was a kid before I went to sleep.

My Uncle Sam and I had dinner together that night at my dad's favorite restaurant.

The next day I finished going through all his things. I whittled everything I was keeping down to one box to mail back to Minneapolis. The box included a picture of my dad at the age of sixteen, sitting on the front steps with his father; his 1939 St. Paul Central High School yearbook; his diary from when he was a Merchant Marine in World War II; and his wrist watch.

My favorite item in the box was a picture of him and a friend in the Minneapolis *StarTribune* dated March 31, 1934, when he was thirteen years old. He was delivering newspapers to John Dillinger's apartment building on Lexington Avenue in St. Paul and heard gunshots. He and his friend saw Dillinger and his gang escape from the police and FBI. The picture in the paper had this headline: Boys See Dillinger Car.

My sister organized his graveside funeral in St. Paul and made arrangements for him to be buried in a simple pine box. The obituary was in the St. Paul newspaper, and word spread fast. He hadn't lived in the area for twenty years, but at age seventy-three, he was still young enough for several of his old friends to be alive. It was nice to see and meet a lot of them.

The weather for the late June funeral was very pleasant. The rabbi began the service with a few prayers. Leslie gave a sweet, sentimental eulogy. She talked about how he taught her to ice skate at the local park when she was very young. When her hands were too cold and she wasn't strong enough, he used to lace up her ice skates for her. At the end of the short service, my sister and I dropped a shovelful of dirt in the grave, on top of the casket. Several of the guests came up and did the same.

Three of my old friends from elementary school showed up, and we got a chance for a quick hello after the ceremony. They remembered my dad as an assistant coach in Little League Baseball. My dad would take the whole gang out for ice cream after each game, win or lose.

Before leaving, I also got a chance to visit with a few of his friends. A buddy of his laughed when he remembered how my dad had a nickname for everyone. One of his high school pals told me about the time they invented a fake student and turned in work for him in all his classes. He said they pulled it off for a whole school year.

The next day I dropped my sister at the airport. Our original four-person nuclear family was now down to the two of us.

CHAPTER SEVEN

Goodbye to Roy

DETERMINATION — Practice this variation of the Warrior pose to strengthen your determination to deal with life's challenges. (From a wide stance, place your left foot facing directly to the left and keep your right foot and hips facing forward. Heals are aligned. Bend your right knee slightly toward the right foot. Bend your left knee slightly toward the left foot. Extend your arms to shoulder height, parallel to the ground, with your left arm above your left leg and the right arm opposite of the left arm. Look to the left arm. Repeat on the opposite side. Remind yourself to smile now and then.)

A week after my dad's funeral, the director of the Meditation Center stopped me in the hall on my way to class. "Hi, Daniel, how is your practice going?"

"You know, it has its ups and downs," I responded. "But I have noticed some changes. I don't get stuck in the downs as much as I used to."

"Are you interested in assisting with the next Yoga 1 class?" he asked.

He stood there patiently, waiting for an answer.

"Me?" If someone told me on my first day at the center that a year later I would be teaching a beginning yoga class, I would have thought they were absolutely crazy.

He laughed. "Yes. The first summer session class is next Wednesday if you can make it."

❈

During the third week of that six-week summer session, the instructor I was assisting asked me to lead the class of twelve people for ten minutes. This was quite a leap from my background of teaching adolescents. While teaching middle school students, I had to be super organized and move the lessons along quickly. Being organized would still be helpful while guiding a meditation or yoga class, but I would have to get used to things moving at a much slower, more relaxed pace. At least I didn't have to worry about sending someone to the office while teaching adults. On the other hand, adults were paying for the class and didn't have to attend. Fourteen year olds were required by state law to attend school, so they were a more captive audience.

I found there was one benefit of going through all the pain and difficulty I had endured while trying to learn all the yoga stuff. It allowed me to encourage and understand others who were having the same trouble when they started. "If you have any injuries or tender spots, and if anything I am asking you to do is painful, it is OK not to do it," I said. "If your breathing speeds up, gets jagged, or you can't smile, it is time to release." They returned my big smile.

After that class ended in August, I started to lead yoga classes at the center whenever my schedule would allow it. My back, neck, and the rest of my body had improved a lot in the last year, but when I would try a new, more challenging yoga pose, I would become aware of a previously unknown area of tightness. The practice of yoga and meditation is a lifetime practice with different layers of awareness discovered along the way.

I began the management of my dad's estate, just as I had done with my mom's. As the executor of the estate, the copy of the trust, will, and death certificate once again became the most valuable things that I owned. I still found it an incredible process to unravel someone's life and bring it to a close.

I also continued a strategy that was a big help to me after my mom passed away. Every week I would get a deep, long massage and other types of body work such as chiropractic and acupuncture. Both the chiropractor and acupuncturist were helping me to integrate the grieving issues. Each time I went to see my chiropractor, he tried to correct a misalignment between my shoulder blades, at the lungs. In traditional Chinese medicine, the lungs are associated with sadness or grief. No matter how much he tried, the chiropractor could not make that particular adjustment. It was like the grieving had melted into my structure.

In September I started my second year working as a middle school counselor. I was also in the second year of my yoga studies and started to read more books on yoga philosophy. Most everything I read in the books was familiar. It was strange, almost unbelievable, to hear from others what was already inside of me. A foundation of the yoga philosophy is "You are encouraged to rely on your own experience to verify if the practices being taught are beneficial." This was a great approach for me. The credentials of the teachers were important, but I didn't have to blindly believe and follow what they were saying. If what they were saying made sense, I would try it as an experiment and see if I could verify it.

On a classroom visit, I had a chance to put the practices to the test. I went into seventh- and eighth-grade classes on a regular basis to do lessons on topics such as managing stress, time management, or dealing with peer pressure. The regular teacher would remain in the room and do some desk work while keeping an eye on the students. During a presentation in November, I noticed that the class of twenty-five students was bored and sleepy. Instead of pushing through the lesson, I stopped talking and turned off the overhead projector. That got their attention. They looked at me expectantly. "I can see that not everyone is listening," I said. "Let's try something a little different."

A few of them perked up. "Can everybody please stand to the right side of your desk?" I asked. I waited until everyone was up. "OK, watch what I'm doing. As I take a breath, I raise my arms to shoulder height. As I exhale, I lower them." They tried it. "Good job, but try slowing down the movement and your breath a lot more. See if you can count silently to five seconds as you raise your arms, and to five seconds as you lower them." Even their regular teacher tried it while standing behind her desk. When the students were seated again, I asked them if they noticed any difference in how they felt.

One student said, "I feel more relaxed."

Another said, "It's easier to pay attention."

"That's great," I said. "We'll do some more exercises in a few minutes."

✻

Two months later, on a Saturday in January, the day was warm enough in the morning that it started to rain, rather than snow. A few hours later, the temperature dropped below freezing, and the sidewalk turned into a skating rink. I was in the habit of taking Roy out for a walk every day, so I tried to manage on the slippery sidewalk as best I could. We ran into a dog friend of Roy's, a large black lab, and his owner. As I visited with the owner, we let the dogs off the leashes. We seemed to be the only people crazy enough to be outside. When I turned away from the dogs for a moment, Roy and the other dog charged full speed at the back of my legs.

My legs went up in the air and I landed squarely on my back with a loud thud. Since I didn't see the dogs coming, I was totally relaxed as I flew through the air. As I lay on the ground, I thought I would be in trouble. Slowly, I did a check of my body. At least my head didn't hit the ground, and I could move everything else. To my surprise I felt OK, got up, and walked away. I looked back at the dogs. Getting angry at them would not have made any difference. They were having so much fun and looked at me as if they were laughing. My back actually felt better, and a lightness and joy seeped into my mind.

The next time I went to the chiropractor, he examined my back and found that the adjustment between my shoulder blades had finally moved into place.

"Did the bones just move on their own?" he asked.

"I got help from a couple of friends."

He nodded. "They were chiropractors?"

"No, just a couple of good friends who were helping me out."

Five months after that icy January day, on June 6 of 1995, I took Roy to the specialty veterinary clinic at the University of Minnesota. The end of my second year as a school counselor was approaching, and almost a year had passed since my father had died. Roy was five years old, and I became concerned when he started to lose interest in eating. They did some tests, and Roy was diagnosed with cancer. The vet told me he thought Roy had six months to live. When I got back home, I looked through an old box in the basement and found my 1990 calendar. June 6, five years before, was the day my mom was diagnosed with her illness.

After Roy became sick, he began to lie on the bed in the back bedroom. Before that time, he had never gone into the back bedroom, and even if he had, I wouldn't have let him on the bed. He was not allowed on the furniture. Because of his illness, I was OK with him going on the bed, and he must have been able to sense that. It was the bed I had inherited from my mom. Just as she started to spend so much time in that same bed as she became more ill, the dog was now doing the same thing. That became his favorite spot, even though the bedroom was not used by me or anyone else. I was always surprised to see him lying there when I walked by, with no one else around.

I went back to work in mid-August to start my third year as a middle school counselor and rushed home every day after work to check on Roy. By late August, Roy stopped eating; it didn't matter what I gave him. It became very difficult for him to move off of the bed in the back bedroom. I had to carry him outside every so often so he could relieve himself. Pulling the plug is a heart-rending judgment call. I couldn't stand to see him suffering and wanted to help him in any way I could.

On Sunday, September 3, I called the veterinarian's office. Fortunately he was in that day doing some other procedures and said he had time for an appointment. I gently set Roy in the front seat of my pick-up, and we drove the three miles to his office.

I brought Roy into the office and took a seat in the empty waiting room. Roy laid down next to my chair. The vet came out to meet us and motioned us into the back room. He had been Roy's doctor from the time he was a puppy. I lifted Roy onto the high steel table.

After the euthanasia shot, I tried to close his eyes as I had with my mother, but the vet said that didn't work with a dog. Instead, I held my hand on his forehead for a few seconds. I remembered very clearly that September 3 was the same day my mom had passed away five years earlier.

The first day of the school year was two days later, on a Tuesday, the day after Labor Day. That time of year was always extremely busy. The schedule changes and phone calls from parents were non-stop. On Wednesday, the second day of school, I got a voice mail from the vet's office saying that Roy's ashes were ready for pick-up. When I told the school secretary that I needed to take a personal leave day on Thursday to observe the passing of my dog, she gave me a quizzical look. Then she nodded. Many people at school had met Roy during the time he spent in my school counselor's office.

After work I stopped by the vet's office to get the ashes and drove to the cabin. The box of ashes and Roy's chain collar were sitting on the seat next to me. My plan was to spread the ashes outside around the cabin and to hang the chain on a nail inside the cabin. I thought I would be too scared to stay up there in the deep woods without Roy, but I knew I needed to face that fear as soon as possible.

It was a warm night, so I decided to sleep in the front screened porch. My heart was beating strongly as I lay on the futon. Finally, I fell asleep.

The swirling wind woke me up in the middle of the night. In a way I had never experienced before, the wind seemed to hug me. It was very comforting, like I was enveloped in its arms. The feeling was quite tangible, and I easily fell back to sleep while listening to the sounds of the wind blowing through the trees. The next morning I felt calm and at peace with the world. What I thought would be a very difficult night turned out to be surprisingly pleasant. The fear I worried about was lifted from me and carried away with the wind.

☀

I attended a talk at the center on the night I returned from the cabin. Every Thursday they had an hour-long talk on a holistic health topic. That week's topic was stress management.

"Everyone has their own unique stress profile," the speaker said. "What upsets you may not upset someone else. And how you react to a stressor may not be the same way someone else reacts."

I raised my hand. "Can you give an example?"

"OK, let's say you are in rush-hour traffic. You may get very upset, but do you think everyone reacts this way?"

I nodded.

"Not necessarily," the speaker continued. "Someone else may take a deep inhalation, a slow exhalation, and look at it as an opportunity to play more of their favorite music."

That's not what happens with me, but I guess it is possible.

"We don't know what stressors will come at us at any given time. We can do what we can to eliminate stressors from our life, but they are impossible to avoid."

That made sense to me.

"But what we can do is change our reaction to the stressor," the speaker said. "How we react is our choice."

My third year as a middle school counselor was also my third year of practicing and studying yoga and meditation. Applying what I learned from the practice was still a work in progress. My body felt much better, but during stressful times, the old pains would reappear. Busy times at my job were a good test to see if I was progressing in my practice.

During the second week of school, a week after the night at the cabin and the talk on stress management, a science teacher sent a student to my office during second hour. The student sat in my office, and I called his teacher from my office phone.

As soon as the science teacher picked up the phone, he started talking very quickly. "This student needs a timeout. I can't do the lab while he's in the room."

I started to ask what he did, but the teacher had already hung up. My breathing remained deep and smooth. *So far so good.*

Before I could talk to the student, the hall monitor dropped off another one. "This is the second time this week I have found this guy moping in the stairwell."

I knew from a previous phone call home that his mom had been diagnosed with cancer two weeks before. "OK," I told the student. "Come on in and have a seat." Both of the chairs in my small office were now filled.

"Alright, guys," I began. Then I was interrupted by the school secretary.

She brought in a student I did not recognize. "This young lady is starting today and will need a schedule," she said.

I got up and talked to the new student from the doorway so I could keep an eye on the two students in my office. "Welcome to our school," I said. "Please sit in the chair here." It was outside the door of my office.

"Please fill out this course options form." I handed her a clipboard and glanced back in my office. The boy from the science class was out of his chair, knocking on my office window to get someone's attention who was walking by on the sidewalk.

"Are you OK with waiting to get your schedule?" I asked the new student. "It will take twenty minutes to get it done."

She nodded. "But can I use the bathroom first?"

"One second," I said.

I handed her a pass.

"Where's the bathroom?" she asked.

"I have to stay in the office and watch these guys." I did my best to muster up a smile. "If you can wait a minute, I'll find someone to show you the way."

After I called the hall monitor on the walkie-talkie, I looked up. The secretary led another new student toward my office.

My shoulders tensed and my breathing got shallow. Often with yoga practice it is two steps forward and one step back. Just when you think you have learned something, you find out more practice is needed.

During my fourth year as a middle school counselor, I continued to fervently practice yoga and meditation. Swami Veda Bharati, a distinguished Vedic scholar and founder of the Meditation Center, returned from India for a short visit after a seven-year absence. I attended a Thursday night talk that he gave.

"Be honest with yourself," he said.

I looked around the room like he was talking to the others but not me.

Then he looked directly at me and continued in a gentle but powerful tone. "Be honest with yourself and stop playing games. To do this takes courage."

He's talking to me? He doesn't even know me.

"At least once a day, for a few minutes, be honest with yourself. Learn to accept yourself, no matter who you are."

I continued to listen carefully.

"Meditation is a practical means for calming yourself, for letting go of your biases and seeing what is, openly and clearly."

Meditation is an internal, solo practice. But the practice not only opened me up, it allowed me to feel secure enough to connect with and understand others on a deeper level. At the age of forty, twenty-six years had passed since my parent's divorce when I was in eighth grade. After the four years of meditation practice, I started to see patterns in my behavior more clearly. I became aware of how I shut down my emotions after their divorce. For the first time, I could see that my habit over the years was to distance myself in a relationship when the emotional intimacy got too close. Once I understood this, letting down my guard with others became easier. I started to appreciate more what others had to offer.

Five years after first coming to the center, I found out that the osteopath who told me about the Meditation Center was an initiate in the same Himalayan Yoga and Meditation Tradition and was married at the ashram associated with the Tradition in Rishikesh, India. I tried to look back and connect the dots. Why did I go to that osteopath? Why did I see the article on yoga on the same day as my appointment with the osteopath? Sometimes the coincidences seemed too much to believe.

I even got to the point where I felt that the purpose of my birth in Minneapolis was because the Meditation Center would be there.

CHAPTER EIGHT

To India

DEEPEN YOUR MEDITATION PRACTICE
— Practice breath awareness in all your activities,
throughout the day. Silently count the length of
each exhalation and inhalation wherever you go and
whatever you do. Extend and slow the count to five
seconds in each direction when possible.

After five years of taking every yoga and meditation class I could, I was still on fire with wanting to practice and learn more. My meditation practice time was increasing, and I was burning to get to the source of the practice. At the age of forty-one, in November of 1998, I took a three-month leave without pay from my job as a middle school counselor. I was single and Roy had passed away three years before. My plan was to study yoga and meditation at an ashram in Rishikesh, India, that was affiliated with the Meditation Center. Swami Veda was scheduled to be in residence there. After hearing him speak the year before, I was inspired to study further with him.

Rishikesh has been a destination for spiritual pilgrimage

since ancient times. According to Hindu mythology, many sages and saints over the centuries did austere meditation practice there and reached *moksha*—freedom from the cycle of birth and death. After the Beatles visited there for several weeks in 1968, the town became more widely known.

With all my trip anxiety, I was constipated for the three days before I left. *How was I ever going to be enlightened if I couldn't even figure out how to have a bowel movement?* The night before my flight, I finally had a bowel movement. It did not come out easily and was a very hard consistency. Before flushing, I glanced at it to see if it looked OK. Something caught my attention, and I had an odd thought. Clearly, it was in the shape of a face that I did not recognize. I flushed the toilet, forgot about it, and tried to get some rest until leaving for the airport a few hours later. While trying to fall asleep, the thought went through my mind that I would not sleep in my bed again for three months.

A five-hour layover in Amsterdam was sandwiched between two nine hour flights. I arrived in New Delhi at midnight. The pre-arranged seven-hour taxi ride to Rishikesh capped off an arduous thirty-hour journey.

When I arrived at the ashram, I was shown to my small, simply furnished room in a two-story, dormitory-style building. There was a single bed, a small dresser, and a narrow closet to hang up a few things. A door led to the bathroom that was shared with the room next door. After I got settled in and took a short nap, I headed to the lunchroom. There were lush gardens everywhere I looked. I stopped to glance at a chalkboard with a daily schedule of the yoga and meditation classes. Swami Veda was scheduled to give a talk that night.

The dining area could hold about fifty people but was only half-full. There were three long tables with chairs on each side. The short line for the large bowls of rice, sabzi (a vegetable dish made in this case with peas, cauliflower, and tomatoes), and dal (lentil soup) moved quickly. Some people chatted softly as they ate. Others ate in silence. The people in silence wore a badge with the words "Silence Practice." I was relieved to find that there would be some decent food.

Several people looked like they were from India. But most of the guests looked like they were from various countries around the world, like a whole United Nations in one room. There was a large age range, from young adults to seniors. On my way out, my eyes stopped at an older man across the room with glasses and an orange wool cap. Our eyes met for a glance. I continued out of the room and headed down to the nearby Ganges River for a walk. *Who was that older guy in the lunchroom?* The one glance told me so much about him. He seemed so friendly, open, caring, and knowing. It was the same look someone would give an old friend they hadn't seen for a long time. The thought faded as I walked.

There was a nicely maintained gravel path along the river that wasn't too crowded. Men wore the traditional pajama-like outfit called a *dhoti,* and women wore the colorful *sari*-style wrap-around dress. A few people were bathing in the river. The various one-, two-, or three-story, rectangular, concrete buildings along the way were used for houses, a school, and what looked like other ashrams. They were decorated in all kinds of symbols and colors. Children were playing cricket. Occasionally an abandoned dog or stray pig would pass by. Loud Hindu music was blaring from various speakers in the buildings. A pungent, burnt smell was in the air, perhaps from a nearby factory. Across the river was a large nature reserve where wild elephants and large rhesus monkeys could be seen if you looked very closely for a few minutes.

At the end of my short walk along the Ganges, I was met on the steps that led back to the ashram by a female swami. She had shoulder-length, black hair and was about fifty years old. I could tell she was a swami since she was dressed in the traditional saffron robes. She asked, "Are you Daniel?"

"Yes."

"The yoga teacher from Minneapolis?"

I nodded and held out my hand in greeting.

She ignored my hand and placed her hands together in front of her chest, in the traditional namaste position. She closed her eyes and kept her hands together as she mumbled some sort of prayer and soft chanting. She opened her eyes. "Are you single, and how old are you?"

I paused, shrugged my shoulders, and answered her questions.

She continued. "Due to health concerns, Swami Hari came down from the mountains today. I think he could benefit from some yoga therapy." She stopped talking and looked at me. "Can you help?"

Yoga had helped me so much that I was very passionate to share it with anyone, even though I never heard of Swami Hari.

"I would be happy to do what I could," I replied.

"Great, meet us in the upstairs classroom at 3:00 p.m."

She turned around quickly and walked away.

☀

When I met them a couple of hours later in the private yoga room, I immediately recognized Swami Hari as the person I saw earlier in the day in the lunchroom. He looked to be in his sixties and was also dressed in the saffron robes of the Himalayan monk.

The female swami introduced me. "This is Daniel. He is forty-one years old and single. Should he get married or renounce?"

I took a step back and opened my eyes wide in shock, but I think it surprised him even more. He raised his eyebrows, tilted his head, and looked curiously from me to her, but didn't answer. *Perhaps he didn't understand English?*

The female swami left the room. I got a chair for myself and offered one to Swami Hari. His expression said, "What am I getting myself into?"

We faced each other in the chairs, a few feet apart, and started on the gentle yoga and breathing exercises. He followed what I was doing as I went through the joints and glands routine that I learned my first day at the Meditation Center, five-and-a-half years before.

After about an hour, we ended the session, and I got up to leave. Instead of standing up and joining me, Swami Hari remained seated and closed his eyes. I felt inclined to remain and join him, so I sat back down, closed my eyes, and started my meditation practice. The joyful feeling subtly emanating from him was boundless. My shoulders relaxed, my breath smoothed out, and a small smile was on my face. Feeling happy was easy in his presence. Any worries or cares seemed to evaporate. I felt like a kid again, simply enjoying life.

Maybe thirty minutes passed, and I got up to leave. When he heard me get up, he gave a big thunderous laugh. We gave each other the namaste gesture and I headed for the door. As I turned back for a moment before leaving the room, he took off his glasses to clean them. This stopped me in my tracks. His face was identical to the one I clearly saw in my bowel movement two days before. I didn't share this with anyone because it seemed too weird.

The next day, I got up for the 6:00 a.m. group meditation practice. After breakfast, I took a longer walk along the river, farther than the day before. The path ended and merged with a busy street after about a mile. I stopped walking and observed the hectic scene. The two-lane, crumbling road was packed with people, cars, and large trucks. The sound of car horns was constant. Cows freely wandered around. One guy with a patch over his eye was struggling to push a heavy wheel barrow piled high with large boxes. A barefooted man slowly pulled a large cart weighted down with all sorts of spare metal parts. Another guy balanced a heavy load of bricks on his head. Across the street was a large community of dilapidated metal shacks. Down the road, off to the side, pigs rolled in a large pile of garbage, mostly consisting of plastic bottles and plastic bags. I tried to absorb the scene, but there was nowhere in my brain to put it. It was unlike anything I had seen before. I turned back to the ashram.

Swami Hari and I met again before lunch and repeated the same yoga routine as the day before.

Later that afternoon, before dinner, Swami Hari and I went for a walk along the river. He walked slowly and would often stop to catch his breath. He didn't speak much English, so we didn't talk a lot. I tried asking him some questions.

"How was lunch, Swami Hari?"

He replied, "A little bit alright."

"Isn't the river pretty?"

"A little bit alright."

He would say the expression with a little nod of approval, as if he was enjoying and completely satisfied with whatever he was eating, watching, or doing. Perhaps it was a prescription for how to live one's life. It fit perfectly into the philosophy of surrender that is adopted when one becomes a swami.

A swami in the Himalayan Tradition is a monk, but not of a religious order. They renounce their attachment to the world, but do not run away from the world. They devote their lives to serving others and often develop projects that are intended to relieve the suffering of others. Renouncing means not being attached to the results of their efforts. Another favorite expression of Swami Hari that described this non-attachment was: "If it happens, good; if it doesn't, double good." A real swami is considered a master of self, which means they have attained a level of mastery in their practice.

Over the next three months, Swami Hari and I sat together in meditation practice twice a day, took a daily walk along the Ganges, and practiced the joints and glands exercises once a day. We became good friends and talked more as he learned more English. I couldn't figure out how his English improved so fast, but when he would lay on his back for the guided relaxation practice, he would always point to the English dictionary to be placed on his stomach. He would laugh and give credit to that practice for his quick learning.

Swami Hari also asked me to accompany him to the local hospital for his appointments. The doctors finally figured out he had a lung problem. He was diagnosed with emphysema and was at about 35 percent lung capacity.

When the three months of my scheduled trip were up, we parted ways. I was due back to my job in Minneapolis. Swami Hari and a group of the ashram workers and residents waved goodbye to me at the ashram gate as my taxi to the airport pulled away. As far as I knew, I would never see Swami Hari again.

※

Adjusting back to my job was difficult. Educational jargon such as IEP, PDP, inquiry-centered, differentiated curriculum, and data-driven action plan suddenly seemed so foreign. And I couldn't understand why everyone was so upset and complaining all the time. My colleagues and I had nice jobs, cars, places to live, access to good healthcare, and enough food. In India there were so many needy people living in shacks or on the streets, with many obvious untreated medical conditions. Many were begging to get enough food and trying to work incredibly strenuous labor jobs. Something inside of you changes forever when you see this kind of devastating poverty up close. Nothing in my life ever seemed quite the same again.

Two months after I returned to Minneapolis, on a beautiful spring day, I was sitting in my school counselor's office. In between visits from students, I glanced out the window and started daydreaming about those walks along the Ganges. The vibration from my cell phone snapped me out of my daze.

The director of the Meditation Center was on the line. "Swami Hari is in the area." A wealthy donor brought him to Minneapolis for medical treatment.

"Are you serious? The Swami Hari I met in India?"

"Yes, that Swami Hari," he responded. "Since you're the only one in the area who knows him, can you pick him up on Thursday and bring him to the center?" They had him scheduled to give a talk.

When he opened the door to the house where he was staying, he greeted me with his big laugh, and I was all smiles. Five months had passed since we had met for the first time.

"How was your flight?" I asked.

"A little bit alright."

"I am going back to India with you," I blurted out. I surprised myself. It was nothing I planned to say.

He nodded and also looked a bit surprised, but didn't say anything.

He sat in the front seat of my rusty pick-up truck, and I showed him how to buckle his seat belt. While on the hour-long drive to the Meditation Center for his scheduled talk, he looked around. "The cars drive fast," he said. "And everything clean and good order."

He was new to the country, so everything he could see from the car window was new to him. The shock I had felt on my first trip to India was still fresh in my mind.

Ten minutes of silence passed.

He spoke first. "You should get married."

I was surprised that he remembered our first conversation, and even more surprised that he answered the question that was asked of him the first time we met. If he hadn't been such a good friend, I might have told him to mind his own business. But no words came to mind. Instead, I sat in silence and concentrated on driving.

He continued. "My master give me big project to complete. Now I add your marriage to the list."

Swami Hari's master was Swami Rama, who brought the Himalayan Tradition to the United States in 1969. To show that yoga is a science, shortly after arriving in the US, he submitted himself as the subject in all sorts of mind-body research experiments at the Menninger Foundation in Topeka, Kansas. He showed, under laboratory conditions, that many human biological responses that were previously thought to be involuntary, are actually voluntary. For example, he was able to raise and lower his heart rate and hand skin temperature at will. The results of the research are in the *World Book Science Annual* of 1974 and several other well-known publications. Swami Rama founded many yoga centers around the world. He was very interested in exploring how the eastern and western medical systems could be merged. Eventually he ended up establishing a medical center that included a huge hospital and medical school. The hospital served needy people from the remote areas of northern India.

"But why do you want to help me?" I asked.

"Your parents are both gone. I am your friend, and now it is my job to see you marry. Marriage is good thing. You don't know what things can come in life, and it is nice to have a partner."

"Hopefully, this will be better than the Jewish Dating Service." I laughed and glanced over. He looked puzzled by what I said. "Not important," I told him. In my late twenties, after I moved back to Minneapolis from Texas, I joined the service for a few months. My overly picky dating checklist sabotaged every first date. I didn't like it if she wore make-up or glasses, and she had to be very fit. She had to love camping and the outdoors, eat only vegetarian food, be kind and gentle, not bossy, and definitely not too religious. Living in the city of Minneapolis, not the suburbs, was a must.

When I glanced over again he looked to be in deep thought. We drove in silence for a few more minutes, and for some reason, all I could think of was the bowel movement incident from the night before my first trip to India. I never mentioned it to anyone, but now, for some reason, I had to share it. "Before I left home for India last time, I was constipated." He looked confused, so I put it in a different way. "I couldn't go to the bathroom, and when it did come out, it looked like you." I kept my eyes on the road and thought he would be upset. All he did was respond with his loud cackling laugh.

As we pulled off the University Avenue exit from the highway, he noticed all the young people walking to class at the University of Minnesota. He spoke softly to himself. "Oh, baba, with all these female, how has he not found wife?"

To start his presentation at the center, he led a thirty-minute silent meditation. Everyone seemed to be enjoying themselves. There was a palpable stillness among the thirty people in the room. He probably would have kept going for the whole hour and a half, but we arranged ahead of time for me to tap his hand when thirty minutes was up.

"My brothers and sisters, I only know three words," he said. "Yes, no, and maybe." Everybody laughed along with him. "How will I talk for an hour?" He closed his eyes and said some prayers and chants for a minute as everybody watched and listened. "I don't know anything," he said. "My home is in the forest, 2,000-meter elevation. Good for meditation." He paused, closed his eyes again for a few seconds, and continued. "My master, Swami Rama, tell me many years before, that someday I visit all his centers in the USA. Here I am." His big laugh flowed naturally.

"Often people come to see me when I live in the forest. They ask many questions. One guy ask why I am a monk. I answer, why you want to disturb me? I am enjoy myself."

Swami Hari paused and closed his eyes again before continuing. "The guy keep asking me why I am monk. I answer: Because I want to know the truth. Then he say: I also want to search God. I answer: It is impossible to search for what we have not lost." He raised his palms-up hands in a gesture. "Is this not foolishness?" He again gave his loud infectious laugh and everybody couldn't help but join in.

He went on to give a talk for an hour. It was a resounding success. He was a remarkable meditation practitioner and was considered a master from those who had a chance to sit with him. Afterward he told me that he was listening to what he was saying and enjoying it, but didn't know where the words came from.

The next day at work, my surprised principal reluctantly signed my leave of absence form for the following school year. I thanked her profusely and assured her I would do everything I could to help orient the next counselor. This had been my first job as a school counselor, and I was tremendously grateful for the opportunity to have worked at Anthony Middle School for the previous six years. The teachers' union contract gave me the right to take a leave without pay for a year if I gave the district enough warning. The contract also gave me the option to contribute to my pension so the year of leave would count as a year of service. I would retain my district seniority, but be released from my current position. That was fine with me. After fourteen years in the district, I didn't think I would ever be back.

Swami Hari ended up staying in Minneapolis for the next several months through the spring, summer, and early fall. Because I had the summer off from work, I had the time to show him around the city, help him set up an email account, and schedule his appointments. Over that summer, I became busier and busier. As more people heard about him, more people wanted to see him. Assisting him became almost a full-time volunteer job. His email account got more and more mail, and he got invitations to travel all over the United States.

He never asked anyone for money, but many people who came to his talks or met privately with him gave him donations. Every time someone gave him money, he would pass it on to me. I didn't know what else to do with it, so I brought it home and put it under my meditation cushion. By the time we left for India that fall, at the end of his first visit to the US, the donations totaled $10,000. Swami Hari asked me to carry the money back to India for him.

To fund my own travels for the year, before going back to India with Swami Hari, I sold my condominium and car. Anything else I owned that I wasn't bringing on the trip, I gave away. There was a feeling of lightness about doing this, but also a little fear, since I suddenly felt so untethered.

Since this was my second trip to India in a year, I knew what to pack and bring. My hair was cut very short; I wore quick drying clothes; checked in a duffel bag; and only carried a fanny pack. When the flight attendant took my boarding pass, she commented, "Now there's a guy who knows how to travel."

☀

Swami Hari was sick during that flight back to India and was very unstable on his feet when we landed in New Delhi. The lung issue was causing him more frequent fevers. He found a seat in the airport waiting area while I gathered the luggage. We walked slowly as I supported him and pulled our luggage cart toward the taxi area.

We stayed in Delhi for the first night with some friends of Swami Hari, and the next day he asked some people he knew to show me the famous tourist spots. The $10,000 in cash was still in the zippered pocket of my cargo pants. I was worried about pickpockets. Everywhere we went I kept my hand and mind on my pocket, so it was difficult to enjoy the tour. Carrying that money became a burden for me. So many people gave the heartfelt donations that I felt a great obligation to take care of it.

When we arrived back in Rishikesh after our one night stay in Delhi, it was like going home to old friends. Many of the staff and residents I met the previous trip were there to greet us. After a few days, Swami Hari decided what to do with the money and relieved me of having to carry it around. He planned to use the money to start a school and vocational training program for villagers near the remote Himalayan region where he grew up. Free, quality education in the area was not readily available. The $10,000 was enough to get the project started.

On this trip, I only stayed in Rishikesh a few days. To thank me for all the help I gave him the previous summer and on the plane flight back, Swami Hari invited me to visit his ashram in the Himalayas. He insisted that he would cover all expenses, and I could stay as long as I liked. Tarkeshwar Ashram was a well-known, ancient holy Shiva shrine at about 6,500 feet in the high Himalayan foothills.

An older, Indian couple who were friends with Swami Hari offered me a ride to Tarkeshwar. They were going for one night only. A woman from the Netherlands also joined us in the taxi. Swami Hari planned to come up a few days later for a short visit, but couldn't stay long because of his health. The night before we left for Takeshwar, I had dinner with Swami Hari in his room. He offered me some of the raw hot pepper he had with his dinner. I knew from my first trip that my stomach could not handle eating uncooked vegetables in India, but it looked so good that I tried some.

The next day, a few minutes after leaving the city roads of Rishikesh, we started on the dirt and gravel mountain roads. We left behind the choking diesel fumes in the city, but the dry dust clouds kicked up by the passing cars and trucks quickly coated our taxi. The road was narrow, winding, and steep, and the taxi driver constantly had the steering wheel turned to stay on the road at each switchback. Small boulders lined the outside of the road to act as a kind of barrier, but it still felt as if we were going to slip off the edge. The taxi driver was used to it, but no matter how good a driver he was, the poor road conditions made it a challenge. Often there was a big, newly fallen boulder on the road. The driver would have to figure out how to maneuver around it while avoiding the edge of the cliff and any oncoming vehicles.

The roads were definitely not built for two-way traffic. Cars and trucks would often come from the other direction, and figuring out how to pass each other was a laborious process. Our taxi would need to find a small indent to pull over into until the oncoming vehicle could get by. Every time this happened, I was surprised that there was enough room for both vehicles. The views of the lush terraced farming and distant villages below were beautiful when I could manage to take my eyes off the drama of the road.

I was prone to car sickness but could have survived if nausea was the only problem. The bigger issue was that the raw hot pepper from the night before was working its way through my system. The older Indian man in the taxi offered me some medicine, but it did not help. The loose bowel movements became a mostly liquid consistency. Legend had it that Tarkeshwar is a difficult place to visit. One can only go there if they are pure enough in body, mind, and spirit. Apparently, even though I had Swami Hari's permission, I needed some more purification.

The severe diarrhea happened at the worst possible time. There were no public bathrooms in the mountain villages along the way. I had to ask the driver to pull over every fifteen or twenty minutes to find a place to release the liquid bowel movement. Fortunately I had some toilet paper and hand cleaner with me. When the taxi cab stopped, I would run up a hill and hide behind whatever tree I could find.

After one of these stops, the older Indian man in the taxi touched my shoulder. "Is there anything we can do to help? Sorry you are having a hard time."

The woman from the Netherlands smiled at me. "Don't worry, I am in no rush."

Even though they were very compassionate, I felt bad that we had to stop so often.

When we made it to the last large village on the way, we stopped to buy some supplies. My stomach was aching, and I had to go so badly that I could hardly hold it. At any moment I thought it would explode out of me. As I bolted out of the taxi, I looked around for any place where I could relieve myself. No public bathrooms were in sight. I kept walking very quickly and a group of about twenty people were following me to see what I was up to. To see someone with white skin and blue, quick drying polyester clothing was a rare sight. People stopped what they were doing and gathered around to see what was going on. My head was turning left to right, trying to find anything that remotely looked like a bathroom or secluded spot. This was a busy village, and no trees or rocks were in sight.

After a block of looking, I finally saw a possibility. There was a pig pen in someone's backyard. By that time, I didn't care if anyone was watching. When you have to go, you have to go. I jumped over the fence and squatted down in the middle of the pigs. When the people following me saw me pull down my pants, they knew what I was doing, and were polite enough to look away. If I had to have more humility to visit this holy site, I think that did the trick.

As we continued the drive, I began to empty out my system and the diarrhea slowed down. I became more concerned about dehydration since I was thirsty, out of bottled water, and didn't have any purification equipment for the mountain streams. A light rain started. It dampened and cleared the dust in the air and alleviated my dry throat.

The taxi still was able to navigate the wet road, but I wondered why the driver didn't turn on the windshield wipers. After a few minutes, the rain quickly picked up and became so heavy that the driver couldn't see out the windshield. The narrow mountain road became clogged with mud. Several times the driver tried to turn on the windshield wipers, but with no success. He had to stick his head out the side window to see the road. *How long can he keep this up?* Every time he took a tight turn a little too fast, I couldn't help but yell out, "Whoa!" The older couple in the taxi had their eyes closed. *Are they praying or meditating?* The lady from the Netherlands was clutching her hands on her thighs. I honestly started to question whether we would make it to our destination.

❊

After a half hour more of driving in the hard rain, thankfully, we did make it. The taxi parked in a small open area near an arched metal gate. Some Sanskrit or Hindi words hung at the top of the gate. We lugged our bags the quarter mile to the ashram on a well-maintained path through the thick deodar cedar forest. Some of the bigger trees were sixty feet high and twenty feet around.

We rounded the final turn in the path. The clearing in the forest revealed the small two-story ashram building and covered outside eating area. There were some crumbling bricks, but it had a fresh coating of paint and overall looked to be in good condition. Two white swans facing each other were painted on an outside wall. I immediately recognized them as the symbol of the Himalayan Tradition.

The cook/ashram manager showed me to my small, lower-level room. He offered to boil some water for me to drink, and I gratefully accepted the offer. After a few swigs of the hot water, I went back to my room and grabbed my towel. I walked a few hundred yards up a hill behind the ashram. A freezing mountain stream became my bathtub since there was no running water at the ashram. The cold water was refreshing, but I started to shiver the moment I took off my clothes and squatted in the stream. I walked quickly back to my room and buried myself in my sleeping bag.

Once I warmed up from the bath, I felt much better. The cook offered to make kitcheri for dinner. Kitcheri is a Himalayan mountain dish made of rice, lentils, and some spices that are good for digestion.

The next day I was surprised at how much better I felt. I was a little sad when I saw the people I drove up with set their small suitcases outside their rooms. They planned to leave that day with the taxi driver, who stayed overnight with them. It was a quiet, isolated place with very few people around, so I thought I would be lonely. The Indian couple's parting gift to me was their last bottle of water. "Good luck," said the older Indian man. As I watched them walk down the path to the waiting taxi, I wondered what I was still doing there. Then I reminded myself that this was a golden opportunity to deepen my meditation practice. That is what had compelled me to travel to India in the first place.

The temperature got cold at night in October. In the day the high would reach the 50s. Often it was sunny, but the hills and tress would block the sun, so unless I hiked to the top of a hill, the direct sunlight only hit the ashram for a couple of hours each day. There were three or four guest rooms, but it was a quiet time of the year. Besides the two ashram workers, there was only one other guest. Each room had two or three beds in it. The mattresses were comfortable and each had a thick, warm, down comforter. Even without any heating system, staying warm at night was not a problem. If someone had allergies, they probably would have had a hard time. They kept the place as clean as possible, but dirt and mildew settled in over the years. With no electricity or running water, cleaning was difficult.

I didn't know how long I would be staying up there. That depended on when someone would arrive who would have enough room in their car to give me a ride back to Rishikesh. Until that time, I was dependent on the cook for my water and all three of my meals. The vegetarian food was cooked in an indoor, cave-like space with a fire pit and steel pots. The usual menu was a greasy, but tasty, Indian pancake called a paratha for breakfast. We ate cooked cabbage, white basmati rice, and hot-off-the-grill chapatis for lunch, and a soup made of whatever was left over for dinner. The chapatis were a delicious, simple bread made from locally grown wheat and water. The food tasted really good for the first few days, but after that the repetition got to me and my appetite dropped off. I could see that I was getting thinner.

The forest surrounding the ashram was wild, with all sorts of animals, including tigers and bears. Every day during lunch, a troop of large, gray monkeys would sit in the trees over the outdoor dining area. They would stare at me as I ate. It was unnerving. At any time they might decide to charge, and that would be the end. Fortunately, they never came down from the trees.

A feral dog would often approach the ashram, but the cook would chase it away so as not to attract larger animals at night. If I happened to wake up and open my eyes at night, I would usually see a large rat making its way around the room. The rat traveled along a shelf, a few inches above head level. As far as I knew, it never touched me, but it always looked very curious as it sniffed around. When this happened, I didn't want to look, so I closed my eyes and tried to get back to sleep. Often I would wake up earlier than my 6:00 a.m. meditation time and go to the temple down the hill to sit for meditation practice. There was something about the energy in the place that woke you up, grabbed you by the collar, and pulled you out of bed whether you were ready or not.

The Shiva temple was a short walk down the steep hill from the ashram and consisted of three or four small, rounded, stone buildings. Only three or four people at a time could fit into a building. The buildings were surrounded by the tall, thick evergreen trees. Each building had a shrine with all sorts of holy objects on an altar. The objects included *malas* or prayer beads, bells, pictures of yoga masters, Shiva stones, and other items that were left there over the years. In the evenings, after dinner, I sat in one of the temples for my meditation practice. The stone floor was cold and damp, so I would bring a blanket along to sit on. A group of *pandits*, or Hindu priests, from the local villages would often come into the small space with me and chant their nightly prayers. That only served to magnify the energy I felt.

When I first started practicing meditation several years before, I had no idea what someone was talking about when they would use terminology like "subtle energy vibrations." If terms like that were used in a lecture at the Meditation Center, I would write it off as one of those things that I would never understand. Sometimes in the lectures it was referred to as *prana*, a Sanskrit word meaning the vital life force.

No matter how many times I heard or read about this subtle energy, it was something that I had to experience to understand. When you sit in silence for several minutes every day with your eyes closed and pay attention to what is going on, you become more sensitive to this type of energy. This subtle vibration can easily be missed unless you can quiet down enough to sense it. Certain people and places have a stronger, more focused energy that can more easily be detected. Sensing this energy went beyond the basic five senses of sight, hearing, touch, smell, and taste.

There are other silent phenomena in the world that can be felt but not seen. For example, when someone is intensely staring at you, it is possible to notice it without a word being said. Similarly, if someone stands quietly behind you, sometimes their presence can be felt without a word. If you walk into a room or space for the first time, you might get a certain impression or feeling that can't be explained. When someone directs a very strong emotion toward you—such as hate or love—without saying anything, it can feel like a negative or positive arrow to the heart. Perhaps the most concrete example of this subtle energy is the charged feeling you can get before and during a thunderstorm. Thunderstorms act as a giant battery that sets up a strong electric field in the atmosphere.

After several days, my meditation practice hit a wall. My body and mind got overloaded, and it felt like I blew a fuse. My circuit was not strong enough to handle the subtle energy flowing through it. Tarkeshwar Valley was known for this type of intense energy. Some people said it came from the magnetic rocks or tall trees. Others said it was because so many people had meditated in the area for so many hundreds or thousands of years. It could take someone a long time to build up their nervous system to be able to integrate this type of energy, and I wasn't anywhere near able to do it. I reminded myself to be gentle and that I had only been practicing this stuff for six years.

Because I was overloaded with energy and could only sit for short periods of time, every morning and afternoon I started to take long hikes on the surrounding mountain trails.

At almost every turn on the trails there was an amazing view of the snow-capped Himalayas in the distance. The narrow mountain trails went all over the area because that was how people got from one village to the other.

The next time I was ready to face the chilly water and take a bath, I grabbed a bar of soap and my quick drying towel and found what I thought was a remote mountain stream. It was a sunny spot, so I took off all my clothes, and squatted in the stream as I washed. While in this position, I heard bells and shouting and didn't know what was going on. A caravan of donkeys came down the path. The path was right next to where I was squatting. Supplies were brought between villages by donkeys wearing loud bells. The donkeys were loaded with gear and food, and used the mountain trails a couple of times a day to make their deliveries. They were led by an expert herder who trained them to respond to his whistles, verbal commands, and if necessary, a stick.

I stopped washing, froze my position, and felt the sweaty donkeys brush up against my back as they passed by. My concern was that my nudity would offend whoever was herding them. When the herder came by at the end, he glanced at me with a quizzical look but kept going. I put my clothes back on and thought that was the end of it. But the next day, word about my bathing had spread through the area.

Everywhere I hiked, the villagers I ran into would smile, wave, and call out, "*naga baba*," when they saw me. A *naga baba* is a swami who does not wear clothes because they see the body itself as clothing for the spirit. Sects of them really do exist, but I only saw one or two during my time in India. Most live in the Himalayan caves and usually only join the masses for special holy celebrations. I don't know how they were able to survive in that climate, but it was a great feat of mind over matter. Obviously I was not a *naga baba*, but for the time I was in Tarkeshwar, it gave me and those who saw me something to smile about. The words *"naga baba"* became our common language.

Swami Hari arrived after I had been up there for ten days. I greeted him in the parking area and helped to carry some of the supplies he brought. He slowly walked the quarter mile to the ashram in silence. Often he would stop to rest. When he did, he would look around and acknowledge everything with a smile on his face. Then he would close his eyes to take a breath. He clearly cherished being back in his spiritual home after he had traveled to the US for the first time the previous summer. Once again he became at one with the forest. It was like seeing a baby returning to his mother's arms. That night he led some chants by the fire for some of the local villagers, and I never heard such heartfelt joy.

Swami Hari only planned to stay for a couple of days. Because of his emphysema, the altitude was too much for him. It was a hilly area with many steep steps, and it was difficult for him to function.

By the time he needed to leave, I had been up there twelve days, but was not yet ready to leave. It was as if I was being pulled to stay longer, and I didn't fight it. He told the ashram workers that I could stay there as his guest as long as I wanted.

Before he started on the walk to the taxi, we had a quiet moment together. He asked, "What do you want?" He had a funny expression, as if whatever wish I had would be granted.

I said the only thing that came into my mind. "Only your friendship."

He asked again, "What do you want?"

I repeated my first answer.

The third time he asked, it sunk into me, and a different response bubbled up in my mind. "I am concerned that there is no job left in the Minneapolis Public Schools that would fit me anymore." I didn't know if he understood what I was trying to say, so I continued. "It's not easy to go back to the farm after you have experienced Paris."

He still looked puzzled.

Finally, I came up with something that I knew he would understand. "I don't know how I will be able to do my old job anymore. How will I support myself?" Working in a school setting suddenly seemed so foreign. I knew I could go back to the district and apply for open jobs, but I couldn't imagine there would be a job that I would want to do. Working as a counselor in a large, traditional middle school or high school was no longer appealing to me. The rigid job duties, unending paperwork, and overwhelming caseloads were not something I wanted to face again.

He didn't say anything after my response, only nodded and walked away. There was something magical about Tarkeshwar, and Swami Hari was a conduit for it. He told me several times over the years that he wanted to help anyone who helped him as a way of giving thanks.

☀

After twenty-six nights, another guest came to Tarkeshwar for a short visit, and I accepted the offer of a ride back to Rishikesh. I was filled up with whatever Tarkeshwar had to give and knew it was time to leave.

After arriving at the Rishikesh ashram, I headed straight to my room. A hot shower never felt so good. I stayed at the ashram for a couple more weeks. Swami Hari and I said goodbye and made plans to meet up in Minneapolis in May. Until then, for the next three months of my leave, my thirst for travel continued. During my stay at the Rishikesh ashram, I met several new friends from various places in Europe. They invited me to visit and I took them up on their offer. Wherever I went I continued my meditation practice, went sightseeing, and now and then wondered what I would do when I returned to Minneapolis.

☀

Shortly after I returned to Minneapolis from the trip to India and travellng around, I was asked by another counselor in the district to fill in for the following year while she was on sabbatical leave. The alternative school served high school drop-outs who wanted to come back to school. There was a small staff, a reasonable caseload, and a more flexible approach to the class schedule.

I bought another condominium in the area of my old one and purchased another car. Ten months earlier, I had left my job and everything I owned, and traveled to the other side of the world. It was like I threw everything up in the air, and it landed in the same spot as it was before. Ricocheting back to living in the same neighborhood and working for the same school district confirmed for me that I was doing whatever I was supposed to be doing.

CHAPTER NINE

Everything Is a Little Bit Alright

LOVE — Practice the standing upper back bend to open the heart to love. (Start with the mountain pose. Place the heels of the hands on both sides of the spine, just above the buttocks. Stretch fully upright. Slowly and gently, slightly bend at the upper back, without straining. Follow with the child's pose.)

Swami Hari returned to visit Minneapolis the next two summers, in 2001 and 2002. Each summer the number of places he visited grew. By 2002, the volunteer job of being his manager became more than I could handle. Several people were needed to help with his world travel arrangements, speaking engagements, and other details. Swami Hari and I got together less often. He was very focused on his project of building the school in India and was making good progress on that. There was very little progress on his project of getting me married.

In early summer of 2002, at age forty-four, I interviewed for a school counselor job at a new school that served new immigrants, ages eighteen to twenty-one. The interview team explained that this was the first public high school of its kind in Minnesota, and possibly in the United States. The school was called International Center for Accelerated Language Learning (ICALL). The thought of working with older students in a smaller setting appealed to me. The interview team thought my international travel experience would be an asset and offered me the job. Two years had passed since I returned from my trip to India with Swami Hari.

In the beginning of the 2002–03 school year, we gathered the 150 students into a large assembly space. This was a good opportunity to introduce myself. "Hello, my name is Daniel. I will be your school counselor." I paused as the interpreters translated to Somali, Spanish, Oromo, and Amharic.

"Since I am your first school counselor, I will tell you what I do here." Again I paused for the translation. "I help students choose which classes to take, decide what to do after high school, and deal with any personal problems." As what I said was being translated, I looked around the room. I could feel the energy and power of being among people from all over the world. About 40 percent of the students were Somali, 40 percent Latino, 15 percent Ethiopian, and the other 5 percent were from various places around the globe. Many came from war-torn countries and had been living in refugee camps for a long time while they waited for visas to the United States. They had experienced something that I would never really understand.

"Do you have any questions?"

A male student in the back stood up and asked, "Can I graduate from this high school?"

"What is your name?" I asked.

"Alfredo."

"Nice to meet you, Alfredo. We are working on that." Every time I said something it took a long time to translate, so I tried to keep it simple and to the point. The principal planned to hire a math teacher, a science teacher, and a social studies teacher. Once this was completed, all the required graduation classes could be offered. I worked on the accreditation process. If we got accredited, diplomas could be issued in the name of this school.

"Any other questions?" I asked.

A female student wearing a headscarf, or hijab, then stood up. "My name is Khadija. Why do we have the name ICALL? My friends think I work for a phone company." She spoke in English. After what she said was translated, the other students laughed.

"Hi, Khadija. ICALL stands for International Center for Accelerated Language Learning, which describes the mission of the school."

She nodded.

"OK, time for one more question," I announced.

A young man in the front row stood up. He started speaking in a language I could not understand. The Somali translator repeated what he said in English. "My name is Ahmed. I want to learn English. I want to go to college. Can you help me?"

"Ahmed, thank you for the question," I said. "The teachers here are very good. How fast you learn English depends on how much you practice and study."

He nodded after it was translated.

I smiled. "I know you will work hard and do great."

He returned what I said with a smile.

After the assembly, I walked by the Level 1 English classroom and saw Ahmed write on the chalkboard: "The boy has a big, red ball." He was a tall, skinny guy with a contagious smile and an upright posture.

A month after the assembly, on October 25, 2002, our staff received some startling news. The small plane of the renowned US Senator from Minnesota, Paul Wellstone, crashed at 10:22 a.m. He, his wife Sheila, and his daughter, who was a school teacher, were all killed on impact. As news trickled in, my colleagues were distraught, but the ICALL students had never heard of him. The teachers tried to explain who he was and what a US Senator does. For those students who understood, they were interested to hear that his parents were Ukrainian Jewish immigrants. Wellstone was known as a strong advocate for immigrants in the US Senate.

By the end of October, Ahmed had already been promoted to the Level 2 English class. When I opened the door and stuck my head in his new classroom, he was standing in front of the class and reading something he wrote: "The boy is bouncing a big, red ball at the playground."

One month after the Wellstone plane crash, at the end of November, I heard a story on Minnesota Public Radio about three schools in Minneapolis that were trying to change their name to Wellstone. When I got to school the next morning, I mentioned to the school coordinator that ICALL would be the perfect school to have the name Wellstone.

At the next staff meeting we discussed it, and everyone wanted to pursue the name change. We knew it would be a long shot. The other schools interested in the name change had active parent groups with a lot of political clout. Many of the students at ICALL were living on their own, without their families. If they did have families, often they did not speak English or understand the political system.

Ahmed was promoted to Level 3 English in December. It was highly unusual for a student to progress this rapidly. Level 5 was the highest English class.

I ran into his new English teacher in the hall. "How is Ahmed doing in the class?" I asked.

"Well, he just started, but he has already asked for extra work to do at home," she said. "Even if a friend asks him something in Somali, he will only answer in English."

In January we invited a school board member to visit the school. She had been a friend of Paul Wellstone and confided in me how much she missed him. When she visited the classrooms and spoke to the students, she saw first-hand all the challenges the students faced as they adjusted to life in a new country. She also saw how sincere they all were, and that they were clearly there to make a better life for themselves. The school coordinator and I walked her to the door at the end of her visit. "It would be a great tribute to Paul to have a school like this named after him," she said.

By the start of the second semester, in February, the staff hires were complete, and all the required subjects for graduation were being taught at the school.

We received word in March that the school would be accredited by the end of the following school year, June of

2004, and that we could issue diplomas in the name of the school at that time.

In April we heard that the other schools interested in the Wellstone name all dropped out of the process. The idea of changing a long-established school name to the name of a recently deceased politician was too controversial in those communities.

Ahmed stopped by my office in May, without the translator. "Mr. Daniel, how am I doing on my graduation requirements?"

"It is a little complicated," I answered. "Do you want an interpreter to make sure you are understanding what I am saying?" I watched him carefully for any signs of confusion.

"No!" He caught himself. "No, thank you. Please continue."

"OK, I have some good news. Your out-of-country transcript was accepted. That will help cover a lot of your math and science requirements."

Together we laid out a plan that would allow him to complete the other requirements by the end of the following school year.

In June, during the last week of school, we got a call from the secretary of the school board. At the meeting that night, they were discussing the name change to Wellstone International High School. Even though it was short notice, several staff and students went to the meeting, and we all sat together in the front row. The name change was listed last on the agenda. We all waited patiently for over an hour. Finally, they voted unanimously to approve the name change, without discussion. All of us stood up, clapped, and cheered.

The superintendent smiled. "I've never been applauded like that before at a school board meeting. Thank you all for coming."

☀

One week after that school board meeting, in June of 2003, Swami Hari arrived in Minneapolis for his annual visit. Three years had passed since I returned from my trip to India with him. Shortly after his arrival from India, we met at the Meditation Center during his afternoon tea time.

He told me, "I put in a special request with Lord Shiva when I was at Tarkeshwar. This is the summer you meet your wife."

I chuckled. "OK."

Swami Hari continued to lead early morning meditation sessions at the Meditation Center. A group of about a dozen people came regularly. Now and then I would stop by and join them. Two weeks after Swami Hari told me this was the summer I would meet my wife, I showed up to a morning meditation. There was a new student I didn't recognize. Her wholesome looks and gentle demeanor caught my attention. She came in quietly to the session, took a meditation cushion from the pile, and sat very still. The alignment in her seated posture was relaxed and effortlessly upright.

Swami Hari led the thirty minute guided meditation and then we all sat in silence with him for another thirty minutes. The new student disappeared quickly out the door after the session.

A week later I got a chance to meet her. She and her mom showed up at the center for a lecture. They sat in the row in front of me. While we were waiting for the lecture to start, I introduced myself to her mom.

"Nice to meet you. This is my daughter Nikki," she said. She was visiting Nikki in Minneapolis for a couple of days. They planned to drive to Duluth, in northern Minnesota, the next day.

"Duluth is great," I said. "I will be at my cabin tomorrow if you guys want to stop by for lunch on your way back."

Before Nikki could respond, her mom replied. "Thank you, that would be nice."

I gave her the directions.

The next day they stopped by. To Nikki's embarrassment, her mom talked nonstop about all the impressive things Nikki had accomplished in her life. She was a graduate student at the University of Minnesota and was in the process of finishing her PhD in geology and civil engineering. Nikki was intelligent, attractive, and modest. Her calm nature was contagious.

A couple of days later, I stopped by Swami Hari's room to visit with him during his afternoon tea time. We sipped our tea in silence for a few minutes. I knew if I told Swami Hari about Nikki and her mom's visit to my cabin, he would be very interested. I set down my cup, sat up straight, and let out a long slow exhalation, as if I was preparing for meditation.

Swami Hari glanced at me and took a sip of his tea.

"Nikki and her mom came up to my cabin the other day for lunch," I said.

He set down his teacup and looked up at me. "Nikki?" he asked.

"Yes, she has been coming to your morning meditations this summer."

He nodded. "Oh yes, I know Nikki." He paused like he was thinking of something. "You met her mother?"

"Yes. We had a nice visit and I liked both of them."

He nodded.

We finished our tea in silence for the few minutes until his next visitor arrived.

Three days later, I stopped by again to have afternoon tea with him.

He mentioned that Nikki had stopped by earlier that morning. Often students would come by to ask questions about their practice.

He told me what he said to her: "I think you should marry my friend Daniel."

"Oh my God," I responded. "Did she run away?"

We both laughed.

"Everything is a little bit alright," he said.

☀

When I ran into Nikki a few days later at the center, she accepted my invitation to see the play *Pride and Prejudice* at the Guthrie Theater. The Guthrie is a well-known regional theater and had been the anchor of the vibrant Twin Cities theater scene since 1963. *Pride and Prejudice* was based on the 1813 book by Jane Austen and was a humorous look at a mother's attempt to get her five daughters married off. To play it safe, Nikki brought along two of her undergraduate students. We all waited in the rush line together. Nikki and I ended up with front row, center seats. The students sat together a little further back.

Before the play, we had a few minutes to chat.

"These seats are amazing," she said.

"I know, unbelievable." If I leaned forward, I could touch the stage. "Did you ever do theater?" I asked.

"In high school I spent a lot of time in the drama club," she said. "I loved it. What about you?"

"Yeah, for a while. Fifteen years ago, I had a part as an extra on this stage."

"Wow, fun. So you weren't always Swami Hari's assistant?"

I laughed as the lights lowered for the play to begin.

During intermission, Nikki and I had a chance to talk some more, without her students around. She told me about the conversation she had with Swami Hari after he told her she should marry me.

She was in shock. "Did you ask Daniel about this?" she had asked Swami Hari.

He replied, "How about next week? I can arrange everything."

"Sounds like Swami Hari," I said.

Nikki continued with her story. Two days after the encounter with Swami Hari, she told me she ran into the director of the center in the hallway after the morning meditation. "What are you guys trying to do, marry me off? Is this a cult or something?"

The director laughed. "Don't worry about it. Arranged marriages are common in India, especially in the area Swami Hari is from. Daniel is a nice guy. I hope you don't blame him for this."

After the play, I offered to drop Nikki at her campus apartment. The two undergraduate students drove on their own back to campus. We chatted about how great the seats were and what a fun play it was. We arrived at her apartment and said goodnight.

Nikki opened the passenger door to get out and turned around to face me before leaving the car. "I am not looking for marriage, but I am glad I decided to at least be nice to you," she said.

The next day I visited Swami Hari in his room.

"The time with Nikki went well last night," I said.

He was beaming and nodding to me.

Then he closed his eyes and whispered under his breath. "Thank you, baba."

Two weeks later Nikki and I went out again, without her undergraduate students, and discovered we had a lot more in common than theater. Both of us practiced yoga and meditation, had the same religion, were vegetarian, and loved the outdoors.

Nikki was very busy working on her PhD, but when we had a chance, we continued to see each other. Our favorite spot was to sit after dark on the St. Anthony Falls Stone Arch Bridge, near her University of Minnesota laboratory. On clear nights we held hands and gazed at the moon as it floated over the Mississippi River.

Our first kiss was two months after seeing the show at the Guthrie, on a beautiful full moon night in July of 2003. Nikki was the nicest, sweetest person I had ever met.

☀

A month later, in August of 2003, I started my second year at Wellstone. Ahmed started in the Level 4 English class. He had turned twenty years old over the summer and would be allowed to stay at the school for the whole year, until age twenty-one.

In mid-September, the staff planned a large name changing ceremony. At the end of September, the 200 students gathered together and heard talks from the mayor, superintendent, a school board member, a local legislator, and the teachers' union president. All of them talked about their love for Paul Wellstone and told stories about his life. At the end of the ceremony, the students sang a rousing version of a Woody Guthrie song they had been rehearsing in their classes: "This Land is Your Land."

During the first week of October, there was a loud shouting argument in the student lunchroom. From the other side of the large room, I could see that a Somali-speaking male student and a Spanish-speaking male student were facing off. Students started to gather around, and staff started rushing in that direction. Fights in this school were uncommon, only two or three a year. The students at the school were usually very serious about their studies. But it only takes one angry person to say the wrong thing or look at someone the wrong way.

Before I or any of the other staff could get over to help, Khadija and Alfredo were both there. They got between the students and calmed them down enough that they agreed to go back and sit down. Once the staff arrived, they got everybody else back in their seats.

After lunch, I caught up with Alfredo and Khadija and asked them to stop by my office. During the first student assembly a year before, they were already speaking English, so I knew they wouldn't need a translator.

"You two did an incredible job. What made you jump in the middle of those two guys?"

Khadija answered first. "I come from a country where war and violence were happening all the time. I want this to be a better place."

Alfredo added, "*Sí*, I had to fight with the gangs to survive. It was terrible. Here, I want to live in *paz*." He looked at Khadija. "*Paz* means peace in Spanish."

"I plan to start a peer mediation program here," I told them. "You two would be an important part of it."

Peer mediation was a system where students were trained to settle disputes between their fellow students.

"Peer mediation?" asked Khadija.

"You mean like in the lunchroom today?" asked Alfredo.

"The idea is to solve the problem before it gets to the point of what happened in the lunchroom," I replied.

Peer mediation is used to settle relatively small disputes that don't need to be referred to the principal, such as "he said, she said" or "he took my pencil." In order to be successful, a peer mediation program needs the strong support of the school administration. After both students in the dispute have had a chance to calm down, either one can request a mediation to discuss the dispute directly with each other. Participation is voluntary.

"So what happens next?" asked Khadija.

"I'll show you two the steps and together we will train the other students," I replied.

They didn't look convinced.

"I saw what you two did today," I said. "I know you can do it."

In mid-October, Khadija, Alfredo, and I went around to each class. They did the talking. Khadija started in English, then translated to Somali. "All of you came from a place where there was bad people and big trouble. Some of your families were killed or tortured. We came to this country to get away from all that." Alfredo translated what she said into Spanish. The students in the classes nodded. She continued, "If you want to help make more peace in our school, please join us. Please let Mr. Daniel or another teacher know if you are interested."

Khadija and Alfredo expanded their talks about peace to the Community Education and alternative high school programs that were housed in the same building. They also moved outside the boundaries of the school building and gave talks at three nearby elementary schools.

In November, an associate educator and I took twenty students who were picked to be mediators by their peers to a nearby, off-campus meeting room. We trained several mediators from each language group during the day-long program. Besides role-playing the steps to mediation, a big part of the training was to teach the students how to remain unruffled when talking to someone who was very upset. Even though the two disputants had a chance to calm down before a mediation started, often strong emotions were triggered during the course of a mediation. If handled improperly, the situation could escalate very quickly. This is where I shared something with the students from my eleven years of practicing yoga and meditation. "If you can slow your breathing, relax your shoulders, let go of any tension in your forehead, and talk in a gentle tone, it will help the angry person calm down."

Without a doubt, peaceful conflict resolution was something that could be taught. Teaching peace was not only critical to the school climate, the skills were desperately needed in the world. I ended the day of training with some closing words for the new mediators. "As you move through life, you will encounter many conflicts. Some will be small, some large. Conflicts are unavoidable." I paused and looked at all of them to make sure everyone was listening. "Now you know a non-violent option to resolve the conflicts."

Ahmed stopped by my office in January, right after winter break. "Over break I applied to the University of Minnesota."

"You did that yourself?" I asked.

He nodded.

"Wow, that is unbelievable. I'll help you with the financial aid part of the application."

He nodded again.

"I heard from your teacher that you will be moved to level 5 in February, at the start of third quarter."

By February, Alfredo had done a few mediations. In between classes one day, he was in the hallway outside my office, visiting with some friends. I walked over to greet him. "*Hola* Alfredo."

We stood together in the hall.

"You guys are doing a great job with the mediations," I told him.

"It's fun," he said. "I have a job after school, and I'm trying to keep up with my homework." He moved to the side of the hallway as a group of students passed by. "But I like seeing people solve their problems in a peaceful way."

Ahmed came into my office in March, holding a piece of paper. He started speaking in an angry tone. "I am so upset. Look at this letter!"

I took the letter from him, unfolded it, and leaned back in my chair.

As I started to read, he started laughing.

It was an acceptance letter from the University of Minnesota.

In early April, I received a letter at school from the University of Minnesota, College of Education Alumni Association. At first I thought it was another fundraising letter and almost recycled it. Then I remembered that the other fundraising letters came to my home address. Something was a little different about the stationary. I opened it. The first line said:

'Congratulations!' The next line was: 'You have been awarded the 2004 preK-12 Outstanding Educator award.' Later that day I found out that some of my Wellstone colleagues had written letters of nomination for me.

Two weeks after that, Nikki and I were walking in the woods near my cabin. Both of us were super busy with work, but since that first kiss the previous summer, we had been seeing each other whenever we could, usually on the weekends.

"What do you think of the idea of getting married?" I asked.

She nodded. "What about you?"

"I'm ready to give it a try."

We held hands and walked through the field on the trail by the river.

☀

We ordered rings from a jewelry-making friend in the area. They were matching silver bands with a Star of David on one side and a Sanskrit symbol for OM on the other side. We picked a wedding date during late June of 2004, when all three of our guests—Swami Hari, my sister, and Nikki's mom—could attend. We weren't active in a synagogue, but found a rabbi we liked a lot who agreed to marry us under a *chuppah*, or Jewish bridal canopy.

On the day of the awards ceremony, in mid-May, I picked up Nikki at her on-campus apartment close to the lab where she was working on her PhD research project. She drove with me to the awards ceremony at the University of Minnesota Alumni Center. We had known each other for ten months.

We chatted in the car. "This whole award thing happened since I met you," I said.

She smiled. "I was born in the year of the dragon, and dragons are lucky." She was referring to the Chinese zodiac system, where each year in the cycle was related to an animal sign.

Several awards from the College of Education were given out during the ceremony.

In my little acceptance speech, I said, "Thank you, the award is very nice, but I promise you: There are many, many more talented educators out there. Most labor without recognition their whole careers. Every day I go into work I am in awe of their courage, creativity, caring, and resilience." Before leaving the podium, I looked up and saw Nikki sitting in the back row. I pointed to her, smiled, and waved. The audience of two hundred people turned around. "Nikki and I are planning to get married in one month." Everyone clapped.

During the last week of the school year, one of the English teachers organized a building-wide writing contest on this topic: What Peace Means to Me. A committee of teachers picked three of the best to print and share with the whole school.

We were surprised when more than forty friends showed up at our International Peace Garden wedding site near Lake Harriet. I welcomed the first friend who showed up and asked him how he had heard about it. He said, "Swami Hari told me last week." Others said the same thing. I smiled when Swami Hari arrived, and he gave his big laugh when he saw all the people.

As is the tradition, I stomped on the wine glass with my foot at the end of the ceremony. The glass we used was one my dad had brought back from his overseas service during World War II. The rabbi said, "Your mission is to repair the world. It will be as difficult as trying to repair the wine glass you just smashed."

At age forty-seven, I married for the first time. Swami Hari said afterwards that the ceremony was very similar to the traditional Vedic ceremonies he was used to in India. The card he gave us after the wedding read: "My long project is now complete and I wish you both a happy life."

A year and a half after our wedding, in December 2005, Nikki and I went to visit Swami Hari at the new school he had built in the Himalayas. The school he envisioned had become a reality. The $10,000 in donations I carried back to India six years before had blossomed into a huge multi-million dollar project. The four-story school building was complete and brimming with students in new uniforms. Now, for the first time, hundreds of children in a remote mountain area had access to free lunch and breakfast, and most important of all, free schooling. He showed me by example what it was possible to accomplish in the world.

This was my third visit to India and Nikki's first. We stayed at the school guest house and spent several days there. During the day, Swami Hari would visit with local villagers and take care of needed details in the management of the school. When he walked slowly around the grounds or up and down steps, he used a portable oxygen tank and nasal cannula. At night Nikki and I would visit with him in his room. It reminded me of seven years before when Swami Hari and I first met and had spent so much time together. This time was a little different. We were joined by Nikki.

Sometimes when the world seems really crazy, I think of this expression, say it to myself, and it helps comfort me: Everything is a little bit alright.

CHAPTER TEN

Gratitude and Forgiveness

BALANCE — Practice the tree pose to find balance
and feel grounded. (Start in the mountain pose. Bend
the right leg at the knee and slide the foot up the left
leg. Rest the right heel snuggly on the ankle or higher.
Repeat on the other side.)

Nikki and I used to visit our friend Vimala almost
every week during the summer of 2012. Swami Hari
had left his body four years before, and three years
earlier we had returned to Minneapolis after the year of living
in Panama. Vimala was a longtime student at the Meditation
Center and became close with Swami Hari during his yearly
visits to Minneapolis.

Vimala had metastasized breast cancer. In the beginning,
after her initial diagnosis, she was filled with anger and
resentment about her illness. Her conversation would be
focused on questioning why she got the illness, the pain
she was feeling, and all the things she would miss when
she was gone. Then, at one visit, everything seemed to
change.

She opened the door to her apartment. "Hi, Vimala, sorry to miss last week's visit," I said. "We were out of town."

"No problem. I have been doing much better." She was smiling. "Come in and have a seat." Nikki and I sat on the couch, and she sat in the rocking chair. She smiled between the coughs.

Soft chanting of meditation mantras was playing in the background. Her one-bedroom apartment looked barren. She had given away most of her things. A couch, chair, coffee table, and a few of her favorite books were all that was left. A copy of *Hua Hu Ching, the Teachings of Lao Tzu* was on the coffee table. This was a book on the Tao philosophy. There was also a copy of Swami Rama's *Sacred Journey: Living Purposely and Dying Gracefully.*

Nikki asked, "Does anyone want some tea? I'll get the hot water going."

"Yes, please, there are a couple of new choices," Vimala responded.

The deterioration in her condition from two weeks before was noticeable. She had lost weight and was coughing more often.

"What is going on, how do you mean you are doing much better?" I asked.

She replied with one word. "Gratitude."

"Gratitude?" I asked.

She emphasized each word. "Gratitude is a game changer."

"But how did you discover this?" She had my attention and I was very curious to see what her answer would be.

"I started to watch every thought, just as we practice in meditation," she said.

I nodded and could hear her wheeze as she took each breath.

She continued. "Every time I notice something negative, I switch it around to something positive."

I had known about practices like gratitude and forgiveness for many years. They are key elements of all the great religious and spiritual traditions, and cultivating them is essential for anyone who was practicing meditation. You don't have to belong to a religion or believe in God to practice them.

Gratitude and forgiveness are two sides of the same coin. Feeling grateful opens the heart to forgiveness. Forgiveness, in turn, can only be accomplished if we are thankful for what we have, rather than what we think we are owed.

Many times over the past twenty years, I had tried the practices of gratitude and forgiveness, but the transformation in Vimala was something I had never seen or experienced before. She had such a huge turnaround in a short period of time.

Vimala looked tired and I didn't want to keep her talking, but I had to ask. "Can you give me an example of a thought you've switched from negative to positive?"

She seemed eager to keep going. "Instead of thinking, *I've only lived fifty-eight years*, I think, *wow, I can't believe I have been lucky enough to live fifty-eight years.*"

I nodded and wanted to hear more.

"Instead of thinking of all the things I won't have a chance to do, I focus my attention on all the amazing things I did get a chance to do." She smiled and laughed again, which triggered another loud cough.

Nikki brought out a cup of hot water for each of us with a variety of tea bags. We sat in silence as we drank the tea, and I thought about what Vimala said.

Vimala pointed to a quote by Rabindranath Tagore that she had taped to the wall: "Clouds come floating into my life, no longer to carry rain or usher storm, but to add color to my sunset sky."

She got up from her chair and slowly made her way to the bathroom. Through the closed bathroom door, I could hear the coughing and spitting.

Nikki went over to the door and asked if she was OK.

"I'm OK," she said. "Go ahead."

Nikki wrote her a short note of thanks, and we let ourselves out.

On the way to the car, I began my gratitude practice with a renewed sense of purpose. As I walked, I noticed how easy and pain free it was to move my legs. I smiled and silently said thank you. Then I took a smooth, effortless breath and gave thanks for this healing gift of relaxation and rejuvenation.

While driving on the highway home, another car cut me off at the exit. Normally, I would have gotten angry. This time I let out a laugh and said, "Thank you."

Nikki looked over at me. "Are you OK?" she asked.

As I pulled safely into our garage, I smiled as big as I could and gave thanks again.

Watching the progression of Vimala's illness was startling. The thought of my own mortality, at age fifty-five, hit me in a deep way that night. When I woke up at 3:00 a.m., my practice of gratitude was nowhere to be found. Instead, these words came flooding into my mind: *Wake up, life is over in the blink of an eye. You have everything you need right now. You don't know when this opportunity will come along again. Do what you need to do.* In that moment I felt so vulnerable that I didn't know if I would make it until morning. It was like I was hanging over the edge of a cliff, holding on to a very fragile thread. The inevitable death sentence wrapped around me like a straitjacket and swept me away in panic and fear. I wondered where the courage I knew only a few hours before had gone. The stillness and silence of the night took hold of me as I lay in bed and listened to the pounding of my heart.

At the first sign of the rising sun the next morning, I scampered out of bed. As I admired the summer brightness beginning to emerge in the colorful sky, inspiration and hope once again washed over me. The death sentence on my mind was granted a temporary reprieve. I smiled, laughed, and gave thanks for making it through the night. When I felt this happiness, I couldn't understand why I had felt so scared just a couple of hours before.

While out on a walk around Lake Harriet that day, I reminded myself to be thankful with every step I took. Every breath was a gift. It was a beautiful summer Sunday, so the walking path was starting to fill up with people. Several sailboats were out on the lake. I took a break from all the thankfulness and sat on my favorite bench by the lake. The bench was near the plaque that my mom's friends got for her after she passed away.

Being at Lake Harriet often reminded me of my mother and what she had said to me twenty-two years earlier. She told me she forgave me for everything. At the time she said it, there was nothing specific to forgive me about. But she knew from the experience with her own parents how easy it was to feel guilty with the finality of death. Now it seemed like a prophecy. She showed me by example the power of learning to forgive others.

I put on my sunglasses, closed my eyes, sat up straight, and slowed my breathing. The smells of popcorn from the nearby refectory floated by. I started to count each breath cycle by silently repeating "one" on the exhalation and "one" on the inhalation, then "two" on the next exhalation and "two" on the inhalation. By the time I got to "three," a big horn went off in the middle of the lake. My eyes opened, I took a look around, and then closed them again. They were preparing for a sailboat race. When thoughts come up during meditation, the idea is to let them be and not get involved. This is much easier said than done.

As I started the count again, a thought from something that happened nineteen years before, in 1993, came sharply into my mind. The more I practiced meditation back then, the more I started to see myself as I was, rather than what I thought I was. This realization is one of the greatest challenges a meditator ever faces. Becoming aware of my patterns of negative behavior had upset me. Anger, sadness, self-centeredness, impatience, sarcasm, and arrogance were all part of my personality. A little bit of any one of them now and then is OK. It is like a recipe; In the right balance and in small helpings, it tastes good, but there are definitely times when too much of any one of them is not helpful to me or others.

A dog sniffing at my shoes startled me back into the present, and I opened my eyes as the owner pulled on the leash. Roy had passed away seventeen years before, and I never got another dog, but whenever I meet the eyes of a passing golden retriever, I think of him and smile.

I got up from the bench and continued to walk slowly while silently counting each step that I took. My mind again wandered back to 1993. Even though the meditation practice had upset me at times, I was driven to keep sitting every day. It hurt to practice, but the thought of quitting hurt even more.

In order to continue the practice, I had to forgive myself for those negative patterns of behavior that came into my awareness. I remembered some of the experiments I had tried in 1993 with the practice of forgiveness. At my school counselor job or in my personal relationships, if I lost my temper or became unnecessarily impatient, I would apologize as quickly as I could. Sometimes my practice of forgiveness worked out, but other times it was not feasible or possible. For example, I couldn't apologize to my dad for an argument we had when I was in my twenties because he had already passed away.

I did a google search for Jack Hoff in St. Paul to try and apologize to my ninth grade English teacher, but there were no promising leads. A person was never obligated to accept the apologies I offered, but it helped me to know that at least I tried.

☀

The Rose Garden was on the northeast side of Lake Harriet. I took a left so I could walk through it. The one-and-a-half-acre Rose Garden was the second oldest public rose garden in the United States. The range of colors in the 3,000 plants and 100 different varieties was a feast for my eyes. Many people were milling about and taking pictures. Across the street from the Rose Garden was the International Peace Garden where Nikki and I were married eight years earlier, in 2004. The spot where our wedding ceremony took place was now covered in trees, so I sat on the ground and leaned back against one of those trees.

As I listened to the small waterfall a few feet away, I once again sat up straight and started the count of each breath. The thought of something I yelled out of a car window in 1975 to a high school classmate came into my mind. That's the way it was with meditation. You never know what thought is going to float through next. And often you never know why a particular memory sticks around. Before I became aware my mind had wandered, I replayed the entire event in my mind. The guy and his date were standing in line outside of a movie theater as the car I was in slowly cruised by. When I yelled out the window, "You suck Crane!" the car full of guys I was with started laughing. Our driver stopped the car for a few seconds in front of where Crane was standing. The other guys in the car continued the taunting. Several people in line who knew him also laughed. The hurt look on his face stuck with me.

I got up from the Peace Garden and started the last mile back to our house. While walking, I thought of the time I apologized to Crane for that incident at our twentieth high school reunion in 1995.

Finally, I tracked him down through the large crowd. "Hey, how is it going?" I asked him.

"Good to see you, man." He shook my hand. "What are you up to these days, Danny boy?"

"Last month I finished my tenth year in the Minneapolis Public Schools as a teacher and counselor," I answered.

"Really? I never imagined a putz like you becoming a teacher, but yeah, I guess you would be pretty good at it."

"Um, thanks, I think. Hey Crane, there is something I wanted to ask you about. Do you remember the comment I yelled from a car when you and your girlfriend were on your first date?"

"Dude, that was you? I had no idea who that was." He closed his eyes for a moment. "I was pissed, but I guess it worked out OK. You knew I ended up marrying her, right?"

"I didn't know that." I smiled. "That is awesome, congratulations!"

"Yeah, we have three kids."

"Wow! Amazing." The music was blaring, so I spoke a little louder. "The reason I asked is that what I said was mean, and I apologize."

He laughed and took a swig of his beer. "Not to worry about it, man. You suck too." Then he smiled. "Besides, that was probably payback for when you lost your Honors Pass after that assembly."

He glanced away for a second then turned back. "Listen, hey, I gotta catch someone else real fast. Take care."

I finished the walk around Lake Harriet and returned home to mow the lawn. As I pushed the non-motorized mower across the lawn, I continued to contemplate the process of forgiveness. Forgiving myself wasn't a selfish way of letting myself off the hook. It meant taking responsibility and loving myself in spite of all the faults. Feeling compassion toward myself is the only way I found to develop a real and deep compassion toward others.

After I mowed the front lawn, I continued on to the back lawn and also continued thinking about forgiveness. Depending on the offense, forgiving someone else could be an agonizing, soul searching activity. Forgiving someone doesn't excuse the act, but it does allow the forgiver to move on with life. There is really no right or wrong way to do it, and it can only be done when someone is ready to forgive.

I finished mowing the back lawn, put the mower in the garage, and laid down in the hammock on the back patio. My eyes closed and my mind veered off to a different memory. Six years before, in 2006, I got a call in my office at Wellstone from my graduate school advisor, the one who helped me figure out a plan to pass the group counseling class. This was the first contact with my graduate school since I had finished there thirteen years earlier.

"This is my last year before retirement," my advisor said. "It would be good to see you before I move out of state. But the main reason I am calling is that I am giving a workshop on supervising interns." I had supervised several interns from other colleges over the years, but I always ignored queries from my graduate school program to do the same.

"You work at a unique school, with new immigrants," he said. "Our students could use the kind of diverse experience that your program offers."

He had been such a big help to me. "Yes, I'll plan to attend. It would be good to see you too."

After I hung up the phone, I could feel the grudge I was holding toward that college lift from my shoulders. At the same time, so did the power of the negative thinking I was holding onto all those years. Instead, a kind of gratitude swept over me. Although I wouldn't wish the experience on anyone else, I was even able to feel gratitude for the Incomplete grade from the group counseling professor. She was no longer a university faculty member, but in a strange, roundabout way, she showed me what it meant to be a school counselor. Since becoming a school counselor, whenever a student came to me who was having a problem with a teacher, I would remind myself how terrible the feeling of helplessness was after I received that grade of "I." The group counseling professor held all the power. The students I worked with were in the same position with their teachers.

The next day, the gratitude practice I had started after that visit with Vimala continued. As soon as I woke up Monday morning, I smiled and laughed. Before and after my meditation practice, I gave a big laugh. Throughout the day, I smiled whenever I remembered to do so. After a couple of weeks, the smiles and laughs became easier and less forced, and I felt better. The experiment was working for me, but was it my imagination? On a Google search I entered "science of smiling," and several studies popped up. The feel good neurotransmitters of dopamine, endorphins, and serotonin are all released when a smile flashes across your face. The studies concluded that simply by moving your mouth into the smile position, whether authentic or not, makes a person happier.

A relentless practice of gratitude requires a constant re-framing of your mind. This can be a daunting process, but it is worth the time and effort. It opened my heart to what I had, rather than what I didn't. What became a game changer for Vimala, also became a game changer for me. I told this to Vimala before she died. Because of the talks we had over the last few months of her life, she asked me to give the eulogy at her funeral. I was happy to accept the honor.

The longer I live, the more I believe that the only regret I will have at the time of my death is that I lived with too much fear and not enough joy. Whenever my life ends, I feel like these thoughts will come to me: *Why did I get so upset about that? There was nothing to it. All I had to do was have fun and enjoy myself.*

I am convinced that laughter and smiling are the only real antidotes for surviving the struggles in life.

CHAPTER ELEVEN

Moving On

TRANSFORM, RENEW, AND ACCEPT —
Practice the gentle cobra pose to embrace all stages
of life. (Lie on the stomach with forehead resting on
the floor, legs and feet together with toes pointed.
Bend the elbows, keep them close to the body, palms
down, with hands next to the chest. Stretch the head
forward and upward very gently so you can feel the
stretch between the shoulder blades. Follow with the
child's pose.)

With two days left in the school year, in June of
2016, the principal scheduled a staff meeting an
hour before the students were supposed to arrive.
Usually when we walked in the room, an agenda was handed
out. This time, there was nothing.

The principal began the meeting by asking, "Are there any
announcements?" She paused and looked around the room.

One teacher asked, "When does the bus ride to the game
leave today?"

"10:30," she responded. "Check the email I sent earlier in

the week if you have questions about the field trip. Any other announcements?" She looked around the room of about thirty people and then rested her gaze on me. After a pause, she raised her eyebrows and tilted her head in anticipation.

I almost got up and left the room.

She smiled and said, "Daniel, any announcements?"

Reluctantly, I stood up, moved to the front of the room, and sat down at the table facing the group. I wanted to go out quietly and fade away, but now it was too late for that.

The principal sat down next to me. "Should I tell them?" she asked.

"I got it," I said. I turned toward the group. "Some of you may know I've reached the Rule of 90." My age of fifty-nine plus my thirty-one years in the district totaled ninety, which qualified me for the pension. Unfortunately, the same rule has been phased out for younger teachers.

As I tried to slow my breath, I couldn't quite get enough air. "I couldn't think of a better group of colleagues to work with during my last five years in the district." After the nine years at Wellstone International High School, I had moved to this school, which served students with special needs, ages eighteen to twenty-one.

For years I had dreamed and planned for the day I could take my pension and walk out the door. But now that it was here, the future looked uncertain and filled with unsettling questions. For all those years, I simply had to show up for my job, and I was making a meaningful contribution to people's lives and society. How do you walk away from something that felt like a calling, in the same way that ministers, hospice workers, and even writers must feel?

The emotional pattern established in my first year of teaching in Dallas continued throughout my career. The day before winter break was always the best day of the year, and the day after winter break was the most psychologically devastating day of the year. But during the last five years, when I could see retirement on the horizon, those feelings moderated. Coming into work every day was a privilege, and I tried to savor each moment.

My position as a school counselor put me smack in the

middle of everything that was going on in the school. Students and staff came to me all day long with questions and requests. Now it was scary to think that leaving would make me irrelevant.

"It's not easy to leave a job that you love and can still do well," I continued. "It feels like a piece of you is being torn off." An unshakable belief that what you were doing was making a difference was absolutely necessary in order to keep going, day after day, in the face of seemingly insurmountable challenges.

Two months before, in early April of 2016, I started to take long walks around Lake Harriet to process the possible transition and try to calm the tension headaches and occasional panic attack. On the morning of Thursday, April 21, news reports came out that Prince, the famous musician from Minneapolis, was dead. Word spread fast around the school. As I walked around the lake that night, I recalled hearing my first Prince song on the way to meet my principal in Dallas. Prince's recording career spanned the whole length of my career in education. Now he was gone.

"I've worked at six different schools over the years," I told the group. "Each one has been like a chapter in my life. But it cannot be denied that there are fewer chapters left in my book." One teacher got up to leave. "Sorry if I am boring anyone," I told the group. "I'll make this fast." The teacher stopped and said, "Just going to the bathroom, be right back. "

The principal said, "We still have some time. Does anyone have a question for Daniel?" I knew that the teachers were usually anxious to get to their classrooms in the morning, but they looked relaxed and settled in.

There were a lot of younger teachers on the staff. One of them asked, "What kind of changes have you seen since you started?"

"Ah, good question," I said. "As you can probably guess, there have been massive changes in the technology and data systems."

In 1985, my first year in the Minneapolis Public Schools, student schedules were hand written. Movies were still shown on reel-to-reel projectors, ditto machines were used to make copies, and overhead projectors with plastic transparencies were state of the art. The biggest change was in the demographics. The percentage of students whose first language is not English soared from 2 percent to about 25 percent. In my first year, the district was 60 percent white, and 40 percent students of color, mostly African American. In thirty-one years, those statistics flip-flopped. When I left, about 70 percent of the students were of color. A willingness to embrace these changes was essential to surviving in the job.

"OK, time for one more question," the principal announced. "Anyone?"

Another new teacher raised her hand. "Why are you retiring if you love it so much?" she asked. "Like, you seem so young," she said.

"Thanks," I replied. "It's a really hard thing to figure out, and I kept going back and forth." Mostly I wanted to leave when I was still excited and positive about life. I was a little tired, but rather than retirement, I looked at it as a transition to something different. Over the years, I had seen a few teachers stay too long. They became ornery, impatient, and cynical. I did not want to be one of them.

"But what will you do?" the new teacher asked.

"Oh, well, they send old teachers out to a farm and you can roam around wherever you want."

"Very funny," she said. "Really, do you have any plans?"

"My wife Nikki and I are looking at some traveling. Number one on the list is to visit Tibet." In between trips, my plan was to offer more meditation classes in the community and continue to offer biofeedback sessions at the Meditation Center. I wanted to be open to whatever came up.

"Alright, thanks Daniel," the principal said as she stood up. "We all wish you the best of luck." There was a smattering of applause as the teachers rushed off to their rooms. A couple of people stayed after to shake my hand and offer their congratulations.

On the last day of school, a few people dropped off cards at my office. Written on my favorite was, "Congratulations, Graduate!"

That night of the last day of school, I took my usual walk around Lake Harriet. There were so many thoughts streaming through my mind. I calculated that I taught or counseled more than 7,500 students since that first year in Dallas. But even after all those years, the memories from my first teaching year in Dallas remained embedded deep in my mind. For the next twenty years after leaving Dallas, I had a recurring nightmare of yelling at a class that would not quiet down. Even though I remembered all their names, for many years I had no way of contacting any of the students from that class.

That all changed a month after I took my pension. I was able to find two of my favorite students from Dallas on Facebook. It felt like I had found long lost children of mine. I was fifty-nine years old and they were forty-seven. Both of the students I found had careers, families, and were doing well. They were very surprised to hear from me.

After a search of some old boxes in my basement, I shared the official class photo that was taken in the spring of 1983. They immediately posted it on their pages. Curtis wrote, "But Mr. Hertz, we gave you such a hard time." He was the student who asked me for help with his math assignment that day after school. I posted back, saying, "I am sorry I didn't have the skills back then to help more, and I'm sorry for all the mistakes I made as a new teacher."

The other student I found, Larena, posted a long essay about what she remembered from that year. She wrote, "I remember the time Mr. Hertz sent me out of class and how red with anger he turned when I argued with him." She also wrote, "I remember winning the school-wide speech contest that year. Mr. Hertz, thank you for the help you gave me on that project."

In April of 2018, almost two years after I found them on Facebook, I was on the campus of Minneapolis Community and Technical College. I had just finished teaching a spring semester meditation class and was heading toward the parking ramp. A familiar voice shouted after me. "Daniel, Daniel!" I couldn't quite place it, but when I turned around I recognized him right away. The gangly nineteen-year-old had turned into a full grown adult. Ahmed and I gave each other a big hug.

"What are you doing on campus?" I asked.

"I teach economics here while finishing my PhD dissertation this summer," he said.

I laughed. "Your PhD? You've come a long way, my friend. What was it, fifteen years ago and you didn't know any English?"

He smiled and nodded. "I have to get to class, but let's have lunch next time you are on campus."

"OK, maybe next Tuesday," I said. "I'll email you."

One of my greatest joys is to run into former students.

☀

There were so many highlights in the thirty-six years since I first stepped foot into that Dallas classroom. I found the Meditation Center, met Swami Hari, and married Nikki. But the five year period, from 1990–95, was unlike any other time. I lost my mother, father, and Roy. Without a doubt, the most profound events of my life were being with each of them at the moments they passed away.

The difference between life and death is such a fragile line. One moment they were there, and the next they were gone. Things that were thought to be so important suddenly became so small when compared to the enormity of death. The finality and mystery of it left many more questions than answers. Was death the end or only a pause in the beginning of a new adventure?

The connection between Roy and my mom convinced me that if the love is strong enough, anything is possible. Like birth, death is about love. Only after my parents' deaths did I truly appreciate and understand the unconditional love they had for me. The love and gratitude I had for them increased as time went by.

I continue to marvel at the courage both my parents displayed as they moved through their diagnoses and illnesses. Everyone has that well of courage buried inside of them. When you need it the most, it will be there.

My parents showed me in their deaths that all pain and suffering eventually end. Change is the one thing in life that is certain to happen, and there is no way to resist it. Once I accepted that, the healing began.

Coordinate all yoga poses with slow, smooth, diaphragmatic breathing. Learn under the direction of a qualified teacher. Each pose has variations that can be adapted to any physical limitation.

My Bar Mitzvah, 1970

My sixth grade class in Dallas, 1982–83

Larry with his cross-age tutoring buddy, 1985

Roy and I, 1991

After I received the Outstanding
Educator Award, 2004

Our Wedding, 2004

*Nikki and I aboard the RV Urraca
in the Panama Canal, 2008*

Some students and I at the Peace Pole in front of
Wellstone International HIgh School, 2010

Acknowledgments

The idea for this book came into my mind while sitting for a full moon meditation on Guru Purnima in July of 2017. First thing the next morning I checked the website of the Loft Literary Center in Minneapolis. A year-long memoir writing workshop was scheduled to start in a few months. What great timing! The members of that 2018 workshop gave me so much help and support throughout the year. I couldn't have done it without them. Here they are, in alphabetical order by first name: Alan Turkus, Amy Stonestrom, Anna Peterson, Barbara Rudnicki, Elisabeth Samson Lee, Jim Moen, Judy Hawkinson, Kelly Westhoff, Madelon Sprengnether, Pamela Smith, and Ryan Atwell. The guidance of instructor Nicole Helget was indispensable. Jennifer Dodgson, Education Program Director at the Loft, was instrumental in getting this workshop up and running.

Madelon Sprengnether took time out of her busy schedule in the summer of 2019 to write a great foreword. The publishing advice from Alan Turkus was invaluable. Jason Hertz, Liz Sjaastad, Pamela Klinger-Horn, Micah Weiss, Sheila O'Connor, and Thom Middlebrook all gave super helpful feedback along the way.

Working with Christine Cote of Shanti Arts Publishing was a great experience. Her expertise and the freedom she gave me was a delight. We never met in person or talked on the phone. I am grateful she plucked my manuscript out of the pile and took a chance on it. Her steadfastness during the height of the pandemic was an inspiration.

My wife, Nikki, has been there as a true partner for the last sixteen years. She is so essential to the story that I almost called the subtitle of the book *Yoga, meditation, and a girl named Nikki*. But even she pointed out that having a dog in the title would sell more books.

The final revisions for this book were completed during the 2020 global pandemic. Living in this time has made me more grateful than ever. I am especially grateful to everyone who has touched my life over the last sixty-two years. The support of family, friends, teachers, and colleagues has been immeasurable.

All of us, across the planet, have recently seen many previously unimaginable changes. My hope is that this book will be a healing tonic for anyone, anywhere, who needs it. I would be humbled if it somehow helps one person along the way.

With love to you all,

Daniel Hertz
April 8, 2020
Minneapolis, Minnesota
USA

About the Author

 Daniel Hertz (MS, BCB, E-RYT 500) spent thirty-one years as a teacher and counselor in the Minneapolis Public Schools. In 2004 he received the PreK-12 Outstanding Educator Award from the University of Minnesota, College of Education Alumni Society. Daniel is internationally certified as both a biofeedback practitioner and as a yoga and meditation instructor. He was initiated into the Himalayan Yoga and Meditation Tradition in 1993 and has been on the faculty of the Meditation Center in Minneapolis since 1995.

SHANTI ARTS

NATURE ▪ ART ▪ SPIRIT

Please visit us on online
to browse our entire book catalog,
including poetry collections and fiction,
books on travel, nature, healing, art,
photography, and more.

Also take a look at our highly
regarded art and literary journal,
Still Point Arts Quarterly, which
may be downloaded for free.

www.shantiarts.com

CPSIA information can be obtained
at www.ICGtesting.com
Printed in the USA
FSHW011151300620

9 781951 651299